THE ART OF CONTROL

Developing Your Intelligent Emotions and Managing Your Life

Gerald T. Hannah Ph.D.

The Art of Control Copyright © 2015 by Gerald T. Hannah, Ph.D. All rights reserved. Printed in the United States of America. This book or any portion thereof may not be reproduced or used in any manner whatsoever without the express written permission of the publisher except for the use of brief quotations embodied in critical articles and reviews.

All characters appearing in this work are fictitious. Any resemblance to real persons, living or dead, is purely coincidental.

First Printing, 2015

ISBN 978-0-9969973-2-4

The Ledlie Group
2970 Peachtree Road, NW
Atlanta, Georgia 30305
www.theledliegroup.com

Published by The Ledlie Group.
Cover design by Raffy Hoylar.

For my brother Mack, an inspiration to all of us, and a great example of courage, faith, and service.

You've taught me and others more about life than you'll ever know.

"As human beings, our greatness lies not so much in being able to remake the world – that is the myth of the atomic age – as in being able to remake ourselves."

– Mahatma Gandhi

Contents

Are You in Control of Your Life?   *viii*

Section 1: *Life*

Chapter 1
Michael: When Parent Becomes Child   1

Chapter 2
Julie: I'm Struggling   6

Chapter 3
Sean: Autism – An Informal Perspective   13

Chapter 4
Karen: Has It Together   20

Chapter 5
Emily: Change is Hard   32

Chapter 6
Kimberly: Marriage is Challenging   38

Chapter 7
John: Heartbreak Hotel   43

Chapter 8
Ray: Retirement, A Love Story. (Again)   46

Chapter 9
Mary: Love Will Trump Cancer   54

Section 2: *Work*

Chapter 10
Henry: Determined to Succeed — 62

Chapter 11
Thomas: I Must Lead — 71

Chapter 12
Allison: Single is not Simple — 82

Chapter 13
Philip: Millennial Mishaps — 92

Chapter 14
Sarah: Work and Family, Where Do I Say No? — 99

Chapter 15
Gene: Will I Make the Right Decision? — 109

Chapter 16
Joe: Is It Ethical? — 120

Chapter 17
Chris: Marked by a Difference — 132

Chapter 18
Steve: Faith, Failure, and Fortune. — 153

Section 3: *Your Life*

Your Personal Development	163
Acknowledgements	168
Contributing Writers	172
About the Author	178

Are You in Control of Your Life?

This is a collection of stories about real people in all kinds of situations. The one thing they all have in common is that each person has some level of control over their situation, regardless of whether the results turn out negative or positive. So how should they respond?

It depends. The success of their response is contingent upon their ability to take control of themselves – through their thoughts, their emotions, and their actions.

The same is true of your life and mine.

Life often puts you in situations where you feel out of control. But no, actually, you are always in control of your response, emotionally and otherwise.

How? When you learn the right skills and behaviors. In other words, you become more emotionally intelligent, your ability to identify, control, and assess your thoughts, emotions and behaviors. These stories give you a window to look through, reflect, and learn so you can take control of yourself.

The stories in this book are divided into two sections pertaining to work and personal life. They are based on many different experiences: some from myself, wherein I delve into the conflicts I've seen and worked with throughout my career, and some from several other contributors, detailing their own personal struggles, triumphs, and views on life.

As we take a peek into the lives of others, we can see the opportunities they have. Did they take the opportunity? Or did they miss out? At the end of each story are reflection statements. These statements will help you to decide what you would have done in a similar situation, as well as what you learned from the choices made in the stories.

Finally, we invite you to take a few minutes to explore the self-development exercises detailed at the end of the book. Each exercise will increase your self-awareness, self-control, and social skills, and will take less than five minutes a day. By the end of these exercises, you will begin to discover more about your thoughts and actions, and you will learn how to be aware of how they affect others.

In life we are presented with an abundance of choice. In any given situation, you can choose how to respond: choose to lose control, to drift towards those emotions which satisfy in the moment, but cause lasting damage over time. Or, you can choose to remain in control, to manage your thoughts, emotions, and actions - With practice, this response will come naturally.

You're behind the wheel – Take control of your life!

Gerald T. Hannah, Ph.D.

I'd love to hear from you! If you'd like to get in touch, you can contact me by email at: Gerald@geraldhannah.com. Or visit my website at www.geraldhannah.com

THE ART OF CONTROL

Section 1: *Life*

Chapter 1

Michael: When Parent Becomes Child

In the past 10 years, the number of grown children taking care of their parents has exploded.

"Why aren't you dressed?" I ask. "We're going to be late."

"I don't want to see the doctor," my mother says. "There's nothing wrong with me."

I ignore that. Eventually my mother is ready and I help her to the car. It's going to be another long day.

That scene repeats itself again and again as I try to care for her. It's been almost 10 years since my father passed away. During most of those years, my mother remained active in her church and took trips to Italy and Ireland with her friends.

Lately, however, she has become the main focus and point of strife between my brothers and me. Because I'm the child who lives nearest to her, I've had to accept the major responsibility for her care. In many ways, my own life has been put on hold.

Looking back, none of us noticed. The old frog in the slow-boiling water. My mother's health deteriorated over a very long time. At first, we didn't believe there was a problem. She would call me at night, wanting me to travel the 30 miles to her home to help with menial tasks like finding her TV remote or missing cell phone.

We thought she was just being stubborn and selfish.

Then there were the odd personality quirks. We noticed she began hoarding paper towels, cereal, cookies, and a lot of other things that she didn't need.

"Why do you buy so many of the same thing?" I'd ask, knowing the answer.

"It was buy one, get one free," she would say.

Logic was lost on her. Any seasoned shopper knows that BOGO (buy one, get one) is only a deal if you go in with the intention of buying the item(s) in the first place. I tried to explain that to her, only to realize I had repeated the same thing a dozen times myself.

Time must move faster for her than everyone else. Every Thursday we have a discussion about how it isn't actually Tuesday. She's typically a few days behind.

It's been hard watching my mother slowly and painfully deteriorate. I've already experienced this stage in my father's life. He suffered many years with cancer. But with my mom, it's different.

She's mobile (thank God), but has substantial degeneration of her lower spine. That causes severe back pain, which prevents her from getting a full night's sleep and from traveling long distances. Her judgment is off at times, which can put her in harm's way. Along with her spine, her world is shrinking.

In speaking with friends in similar situations, it seems their approaches differ from mine. For a variety of reasons, they've opted to place their parents in assisted living facilities, nursing homes, or they've even moved their parents in with themselves.

Everyone who's experienced it will tell you there really isn't a right or wrong way. However, there are two things we all agree on – the guilt and the pressure that comes in caring for your parents.

I struggle to find a balance in my life. I have a full-time job, a loving wife, grown children, grandchildren, and the desire to travel while I'm still healthy and have the money.

But something has to change because now my mother needs me more than ever. For the time being, my brothers and I have chosen to let her live in her house – fulfilling a strong desire she has expressed. But is that fair to our family and to her?

For example, yesterday I was caring for my wife, Brenda, who broke her leg a few weeks ago when she tripped and fell during a run.

Mother phoned, "Michael, can you take me to the eye doctor, I broke my glasses and I can't see to cook a meal or even read."

"I can tomorrow, Mom. But I need to take Brenda to the doctor this afternoon." I hung up feeling guilty, but even guilt can't put you in two places at once.

Brenda had overheard me. "Honey, my appointment is at 3:00. You'll have time to take your mother."

I felt selfish, but the truth is I didn't want to spend my whole day traveling across town and sitting in two different doctor's offices.

Then I paused. "You're right, I'll call her back."

My feelings and emotions are in turmoil about where life has delivered me. It's one thing for me to raise our children and focus all our attention and resources helping them through their childhood, their teens, and on to college graduation. But now, my focus must shift 50 years along the circle of life to caring for my mother.

Sometimes it's ironic, I notice how our roles have reversed as I enter her house to check on her. "Oh, Michael, I'm glad you are here. I'm in a lot of pain," she says softly in a pitiable little voice.

I lead her to the bedroom, "Lie down for a few minutes on the heating pad while I get you some lunch."

Several minutes later I go to check on her and tell her lunch will be ready in about 10 minutes. She says, "Ok, I'll be in the dining room shortly."

I wait and wait, finally saying, "Mom, please come eat. Your food is getting cold." And I smile. That statement rings in my ears from childhood.

"Boys, quit playing ball and hurry into kitchen to eat your lunch before your food gets cold," my mother used to say.

As our roles increasingly reverse, I realize I've become the parent and she the child. It's unnatural and uncomfortable. I feel more real being the son to my parent, than the parent to my mother.

Her short-term memory is slowly fading, and to the point that Brenda and I have to manage her financial affairs, write her checks, organize her daily medications, and assist at her medical appointments.

There are a lot of books on the subject of caring for your elderly parents – trust me I've read my share – but none really get you ready for the despair that comes with that.

The mother I knew is gone and has been for some time now. I miss our long walks, attending sporting events together when I was young, and later, hearing about her visits to see her grandchildren and great-grandchildren.

I feel anger and resentment toward her for getting old – I want to be her child again.

We are the first generation to experience this phenomenon, so they say. People just didn't live this long in the past.

In a clear moment, I just hope I can be as good of a parent to my mother as she was to me.

The time is just around corner when I won't have any parents – effectively making me an orphan.

Maybe I already am.

Reflection

1. Do I do enough for my parents?
2. Can I be as emotionally strong as Michael in caring for my parents?
3. Do you or your siblings have plans in place for when your parents need extensive care?
4. Should I feel guilty about the decisions I must make about my parents future?

Chapter 2

Julie: I'm Struggling

In life, we sometimes arrive at a fork in the road. Which road should I take?

My whole life I've wanted to be a teacher. My mother and my grandmother taught. As a child and even in my teenage years, I loved going to school (I know, strange). There was never another thought given to a different career.

After high school, I attended a small, liberal arts college in the Midwest that had a great reputation for creating student teachers. I wasn't disappointed. Three years ago, I completed my master's in teaching.

But after six years as a third grade teacher, I'm beginning to feel burned out.

Teachers like me are expected to always wear a smile, think happy thoughts, and burst forth with energy and enthusiasm. We have to be strong both physically and emotionally, to handle the daily demands of 25 to 30 kids with all sorts of needs and fears that always require our immediate attention.

I'm constantly thinking about which child will do what today.

"Which child will have another outburst?"

"Which child will have to be removed for behavior?"

"Which child won't understand the lesson?"

"Which child…which child…which child?"

For the first time in my career I'm starting to wonder how much longer I can keep this up.

"Good morning Mrs. Skeen," Alison, one of my students, says as she walks by me in the hall. "Did you have a good weekend?" She's clutching a blue Ninja Turtles lunchbox in both her hands.

"Yes, I did, Alison. Thanks for asking," I respond. We really try to encourage positive social behavior like this.

The teacher's lounge is full of my colleagues. Most of us have been at the same place for a number of years now, so we know each other and our families. I enjoy the camaraderie and the support that closeness brings, and we are also fortunate to have a good leader for a principal.

Leaving the lounge, I brace myself for class. Lately things have been relatively quiet and outbursts seldom.

Then, an hour into class, there's a disruption. Tommy shoves Kirk to the floor.

"Gimme that pen!" Kirk yells.

I rush to the two of them. Both are scuffling on the floor.

"Tommy, get up and stand by the blackboard, now."

I help Kirk up, checking him over head to foot in the process. He wipes away a few stray tears, but he'll be okay. I walk him back to his seat. Then I turn to Tommy. He's standing by the blackboard twiddling his fingers, eyes to the floor.

"Tommy, in the hall. Now!"

My teacher's aide will take care of reading groups while Tommy and I leave the room.

Tommy and I sit on two chairs facing one another several feet from the classroom door.

"Tommy, you know the rules about keeping our hands to ourselves and showing respect to others," I say. "How do you think you should be punished?"

Tommy is slow to respond, "No lunch today?" he asks, looking up for confirmation.

"No, we can't take your food away." I pause and wait.

"Ok, no recess today?" he asks again.

"No, we can't do that either." I stand up straight, hands on my hips in the universal sign of a teacher losing patience. More waiting.

"I'll apologize and say I'm sorry," he says softly.

"I think that's a good idea," I say. I smile and pat him on the shoulder.

"Ok, I will."

We walk back in the classroom. Tommy gives his apology, which almost approaches sincerity. Even that much is rare in children.

This incident was a teachable moment both for Tommy and the class. I'm glad it went well. I have two or three of these moments every few days, but not every incident ends as smoothly as this one.

The rest of the day trudges along as I go through my normal lessons. When the lunch bell finally rings, I let out a sigh of relief. Those who have never taught don't really understand what it's like. Often times you find yourself talking to a room full of blank stares, mouths agape. It's times like those when I really question if my passion has completely left. Other times, it's when I notice otherwise good students begin to falter.

Sophia, who is a B+/A- student, is one of my favorites, but lately I've noticed a change in her demeanor. She seems very tired in the mornings, and for the last few weeks she's been drifting off after lunch.

In the middle my math lesson, I look across the room to find her head down, arms dangling limp off the sides of the desk. I walk over quietly to her and rub her back.

"Sophia," I call, attempting to wake her. "You need to get up. This isn't nap time."

She wakes with a jolt and looks up at me through squinted eyes.

"Sorry, Mrs. Skeen," she says.

"That's all right, Sophia. Can I speak with you after school? Don't worry, you aren't in trouble."

She nods and yawns, and rubs the sleep out of her eyes.

The other thing about teaching that many don't understand is how responsible teachers feel responsible for kids and their wellbeing.

The final bell rings for the end of school. Sophia stays behind as we wait for the other children to leave. She explains to me that her parents have stopped living with each other, and she has had to switch houses a lot – mostly late in the evening.

"Everything's going to be okay," I say, trying to console her. "Can you hand this note to your mommy or daddy?"

Now that everyone is gone I have some planning time.

Third grade is considered by many to be one of the most important grades in a child's formative years, so I take my responsibility to educate very seriously. Each minute that passes is gone forever. The child, their parents, and society – all of them are counting on me.

Lindsey, another third grade teacher, drops by.

"Julie, do you have a minute to talk?" she asks.

"Yeah, sure! Come in. Can I offer you a glass of wine?" I ask jokingly.

She gives a half smirk, one that indicates she's not in a joking mood.

"Julie, I want to tell you something very privately because I want you to hear it from me. I'm not renewing my contract at the end of the year. I need to do something different in my life, and I'm not sure exactly what it will be. I just know that it's not teaching. Too many kids, too much lack of interest. All the discipline issues. Arbitrary curriculum standards. I could go on and on."

"Lindsey, I'm so surprised. And very sorry. I sure hope you've thought this decision out," I say as I hug her.

Then we talk for about an hour before she leaves for home. She has made her decision.

I bury my head in my hands. Lindsey is so sweet, so nice. She seemed so committed to the profession, but she had only been teaching for a few years. Like I said, it can really wear you down.

The news gets me thinking about how easy it would be to walk away. I could travel for a bit, have a higher paying job, be around adults for a change. It would be wonderful.

It would be helpful if my husband was more willing to talk about this with me. He thinks I'm silly to quit a 10-month job that pays me for 12 months of the year. That's the depth of what he chooses to know about my chosen profession.

And then there's my Mom. Talking to her about quitting gives me chills. She taught school until she was 65. I'm afraid she wouldn't understand and would try to talk me out of leaving. Worse, she might succeed.

Of course, there's a case for staying. I do see the impact I have on children's lives. The smile of a student who learns something new. The appreciation expressed by parents and the leaders of our community. And where would kids like Sophia be? Or even kids like Tommy? I couldn't leave behind the hundreds and hundreds of children who need a good teacher in their lives.

My career isn't the only thing I need to make a decision about. I'm almost 30 years old and I would like to have a baby. Three babies in fact. (Preferably one at a time.) It has been almost a year since Todd and I have discussed that. He doesn't seem to be in a hurry. In all fairness, I haven't approached this subject again either.

Maybe Todd and I can sit down and talk tonight.

Reflection

1. How did Julie handle the situation in her classroom?

2. Have you had second thoughts about your career? What did you do?

3. How should Julie start her conversation with her husband?

4. Did Julie choose the wrong profession?

5. Do you ever feel burned out at work? In life? As a parent?

Chapter 3

Sean: Autism – An Informal Perspective

The support and encouragement of family and friends means a lot.

Trees were flashing by as I looked out the passenger window. Across from me, my mom had been trying to tell me something. I don't remember exactly what she said, but I remember the gist of it.

"Sean," she said, "do you remember those tests I had you take several years ago?"

I grunted.

"Well, I've been trying to get some support for you when you go off to college. You've never been without a support system of some kind, so it's important that you have one now," she said.

She paused as if she wanted me to say something. I didn't. She kept going.

"And, well, Western has this really great program for students with learning disabilities. And…well, when you took those tests, the doctors found something. Something that wasn't all that important at the time, but makes a whole lot more sense these days."

She paused again.

"Sean, you have autism."

The car got pretty quiet for a while.

"Huh," I said. Then I turned on the car radio, putting the volume at an uncomfortable level.

***

My assumption was Mom was trying to make some sort of Earth shattering revelation. You know, the kind you could use to start an archeological dig with. But the fact is that I've always kind of known that my brain was wired a bit differently than most people.

I was put in one of those special schools before pre-K, and I didn't poke my head out until after graduation. In that sense, her "news" revelation felt only a little more informative than a news broadcast saying that water is wet.

That's life, I suppose. Some days it hits you like a brick, other days it pokes you in the back with a pillow.

***

There were a lot of things that suddenly made much more sense. All those Sunday morning scrambles to sit at the far end of the church pew. That time in kindergarten when I freaked out during music class and had to put cotton in my ears for the rest of the year.

All those times when I got tired of being in school, excused myself, and spent the next fifteen minutes in a bathroom stall reciting Pokémon evolutionary trees. Little disjointed pictures of my life suddenly came into a new focus.

Her news had a genuine effect on me. It's just that it was more of a slow burn than a raging explosion. And that slow burn was pre-empted by another slow burn. The kind which makes me easily distracted and sends me off to browse Wikipedia.

A lot of my earliest memories involve testing. Going to some building to speak with a therapist of some sort about my life and how I was living it. They'd usually give me some sort of test: rearrange the blocks to form a certain shape or just work out some math problems. Then Mom would have a "private" talk with them that I could overhear. Everybody would use a bunch of words I didn't understand, like "perseveration" and "withdrawal."

I'd later learn that several of those tests would show I had several signs of autism, but I was never formally diagnosed. My mom wanted to focus on the ADD, and while I had several of the symptoms, I didn't fit neatly into any part of the spectrum at the time.

My mom enrolled me in a special pre-K at just five years old. Most of the staff's efforts were focused on strengthening my attention span, which weren't entirely successful. I would go on to spend the next 13 years learning to deal with one disorder, only to find out that I had been dealing with another one all along.

My college years were to be mostly a four-year-blur of last-minute papers, plastic-tasting cheeseburgers, and far too many Batman videos on YouTube. But this was my first real experience with the world while being aware of my autism. I had spent most of my life in a protective bubble, and now I was out in a wider setting with a much wider understanding of myself.

My university had a pretty strong support system for autistic individuals, which was the reason I'd decided to attend in the first place. There I crossed paths with… let's use the name "Kelly." Kelly was trying to organize a self-advocacy group; let us speak for ourselves rather than have some well-meaning folks patronize us. Being new to the whole autism thing, I signed up just to get a better idea of what I was dealing with. Kelly was one of those go-getter types; the kind of person who looked at a problem and started immediately thinking about how she could solve it. Kelly had prepared speeches, flyers, and PowerPoints – I had never even thought about autism for more than a few minutes. That night we talked about organizing informational events, handing out pamphlets, even setting up a movie night.

Unfortunately, it was all very anticlimactic. Due to some backroom snafu – I never got the full details – we didn't get any of the funding that we were promised and none of our plans ever got past the barest concept. What I did gain from the experience was a wider understanding of how people like me are regarded in society. Not to mention a very nice "treasurer" credential on my resume that looked impressive so long as you didn't ask me too many questions.

Years later and last I heard, Kelly had gotten a job in Washington.

Many blessed with the ability to go to parties, or be in large social settings without feeling a deep, existential discomfort, wonder what having autism is like. That's a fair question. I ask it all the time.

Autistics, like anyone else, can't be summed up by a single definition. Each case is vastly different. I'm on the high end of the spectrum, meaning I can act reasonably well in social situations. But there are hundreds of cases that I will never truly understand. Autistics are certainly more complicated than a short soundbite.

One of the funnier things about autism is the fact that even the experts seem to have trouble defining what, exactly, it is. There is a reason they call it a spectrum: the definitions are constantly shifting and being reclassified by academics who presumably have nothing better to do. What's considered high functioning autism one day is Asperger's the next.

Sometimes I think of the spectrum and the academics trying to classify it as a very confused traffic stop. A bunch of dangerously creative motorists have suddenly discovered brilliant ways of driving around, several of which defy the known laws of physics. There's a traffic engineer who has to sort out the whole mess, and he's finding the standard red, yellow, and green lights just aren't cutting it. So instead he invents a whole bunch of new lights and new colors in a desperate attempt to help us make sense of everything, but these lights only succeed in making things that much more confusing.

A lot of people are trying to find the next Rain Man. An autistic ubermensch who they can raise up to the stars, yet keep tethered with patronizing praise and ludicrous expectations. Like they said in *The Elephant Man*, "If you want my advice, he's only being stared at all over again."

I've never really experienced this sort of thing myself – most seem very surprised when I tell them I'm autistic. But I've heard others complaining about it, like that time Kelly ripped Jon Stewart a new one for that special on Comedy Central. I can't really blame them, though. That's how humans are in general. We tear others down to build ourselves up.

I don't consider myself a wunderkind. Who would want to live up to that kind of pressure? I've got talent, sure, but I'm not going to pretend I'm without flaws. I process information several times faster than a normal person, and that's great. But I often spend too much time focusing on the details and not enough on the bigger picture that they form.

I'm great at one-on-one interactions, but if you put me in a large group I'll probably go find someplace to excuse myself. I'm pretty good at public speaking – it helps that I've got pipes stronger than what most people use for indoor plumbing – but it's easier for me to talk to a mass of people than to have them talk back to me, as my brief and ill-considered foray as a store cashier would demonstrate. I am the proverbial deer in the headlights: graceful in my element but of little much use outside.

The way I see it, we all spend our lives playing Sisyphus. Someone rolls us a boulder and leaves us to try and push it up a mountain. We usually don't have it as bad as Sisyphus did. Some people have smaller rocks than others, but at the end of the day we are still responsible for pushing that boulder.

We have to struggle every time it slips. And in the end, we're never going to get it up the mountain. Our problems, our burdens. We carry them with us until we die.

In a lot of ways, life is about learning how to lose gracefully.

I've heard it said that learning what you are is a liberating thing. That's true, I suppose. There are few things more liberating than a handy scapegoat. But the thing is, I don't feel the need to deny what I am. I am autistic. There are upsides and downsides.

In the end, I don't think I have much to complain about. I've got people who support me and I know my obstacles well enough to work around them.

I can see the forest for the trees.

Reflection

1. What is your final takeaway from this story?

2. Is everyone really just playing Sisyphus?

3. Do you think you have a better understanding of what someone with autism goes through?

Chapter 4

Karen: Has It Together

Life throws a lot of issues – and happiness – at each of us.

It's almost midnight as a light mist and fog descends upon Grady Hospital in Atlanta. The stillness is suddenly broken as an ambulance rushes toward the neon glow of the emergency room sign, slicing through the grey. The patient, a 25-year-old male, had been involved in a single-car accident heading southbound on Georgia 400 near the downtown connector. So mangled was the wreckage that he had to be extracted from his forest green Jeep using the "jaws of life."

Emergency room staff rush the young male to a corner of the crowded waiting area. It's quickly becoming a routine Tuesday night at Grady.

"Tonight's one of those nights," one of the nurses says without emotion, making notes in the man's chart.

I move into position to examine the unconscious patient as the rest of the team works on stopping the bleeding and taking vitals. He's lost a lot of blood. His pulse is weak, sinking to 40. The room is roaring, but I stay calm and direct the team. Minutes pass. The bleeding is finally under control. The man's eyes open slowly.

"You were in an accident and are now in the hospital. My name is Dr. Karen West and I will be taking care of you. What's your name?"

"Robert. Robert Brownley," he replies in a weak voice.

"Robert, you've sustained some injuries. We're going to need to run some tests. That sound okay?" I ask, looking into his eyes and holding his hand.

He nods slowly.

In an examination room 50 or so feet down the hall a two-year-old girl is suffering from a 104-degree temperature and intractable vomiting.

"McKenzie has been sick for two days. I didn't know what to do and couldn't find a way here," her mother says, trembling, wiping her nose and face with a tissue that's soaked through.

"Everything's going to be fine," I tell her. "You're here now, and we're going to take good care of her." I put my arm around her shoulder and give it a squeeze.

Robert's heart monitor beeps from down the hall, indicating his pulse has slowed drastically. I rush back down to his room to find my team already in the process of treating a sudden cardiac arrest. A defibrillator sends electrical shocks to his heart while one of my nurses begins (CPR). We only have minutes to save Robert's life.

90 seconds later Robert's breathing begins to regain regularity, and his heart returns to a more normal rhythm. The medical team keeps working. We all know the drill. They are a model of excellent teamwork, and I couldn't be more pleased.

Robert slowly regains consciousness. All is calm again.

"You're okay, Robert," I say. "We have everything under control."

"Great job, all of you," I say to my team, giving a nod of reassurance.

"You did great as well," I say to Jennifer, a two-year veteran of the unit. Just last week she lost a patient in similar circumstances. I know from experience she's still reeling from that.

How fragile life is, I think, as I sink, into my office chair, totally exhausted. Seeing fear in the eyes of my patients and feeling my heart beating fast as my medical team and I work wears you down. But I thrive on such challenges.

I'm about ready to head home, but not before some paperwork and emails.

***

Where It All Began

My three older brothers live in different cities along the East Coast. My mother, Doris, is a gifted artist with an art gallery located on River Street in Savannah. She has a degree from the University of Georgia and is active in various artistic groups and civic organizations (e.g., former president of the Savannah Rotary Club and the Telfair Museum). My father, Raymond, is in his third term as Mayor of Savannah. He graduated from Georgetown University with a business degree and worked for 15 years as international trade director and then executive director of the Georgia Ports Authority.

As a child growing up in Savannah, I learned how to be a lady from my mother and from years at Pope School. I also learned to be competitive in sports, such as tennis and golf. I also excelled academically. My bothers treated me as an equal in games we played in the beautiful square near my house; you might say my competitive streak is as old as I am.

My parents taught us dignity, integrity, respect for others, high performance standards, accountability for one's actions, the importance of education, and serving others.

I'll eventually tell my own children the story about the time my close friend and I decided to skip afternoon classes to go to the beach. Unfortunately I hadn't considered the sunburn.

"What're you going to tell your parents?" my friend asked.

I sat there thinking for a moment.

"The truth. That I skipped class," I said finally.

Mother was in the kitchen preparing dinner.

"Mother, I'm sorry. I made a big mistake today, I skipped my afternoon classes and went to the beach." She listened with both hands on her hips.

"Thank you for telling the truth," she said, and proceeded to ground me for two weeks.

***

Life Changing

Every summer since I was a teenager, my family rented a cottage in Clairborne, a little town in Cape Cod. Summers on the Cape gave me a different outlook on life, new and diverse friends, and interesting new foods.

All of that changed considerably the summer before my senior year in high school when I suffered a severe boating accident.

We had been waterskiing all afternoon. On my last run of the day, as the sun began to set, I wiped out after hitting an especially vicious wake. I landed hard enough that my life jacket came unfastened and I started sinking in the water. Luckily I could swim and I began to make my way back toward the surface.

In the fading dusk light, I guess they hadn't seen me. As I broke the surface, I was struck head-on by another boat. They hadn't been going terribly fast, or so I was told later. Otherwise, I may have not survived. I immediately lost consciousness and woke up minutes later on the boat, everyone looking down on me.

There was intense and enduring pain. I had lost some feeling in my legs. Fear flashed through my mind as I lay on the deck.

I was airlifted to Boston General Hospital with multiple fractures in my spine and a broken right leg. The doctor told my family to expect several surgeries and months of rehab.

"What have I done to deserve all this?" I thought.

After weeks of pondering that thought and praying for the physical and mental strength to go on, I finally realized the only thing I could control was my recovery.

My parents rented an apartment near the hospital and my mother frequently bunked in my room. I enjoyed our talks, card games, and puzzles. I read autobiographies and European history. The days were so long! Nights seemed like days.

I began to meditate. I found calm in my restless mind for the first time since the accident. It truly saved me from going stir crazy.

Back home, physical rehabilitation at Emory University Hospital took over four hours, three days a week. The accident had allowed me to reflect on what was important in my life. What did I want to make of myself? As I read my personal daily journal, I noticed a lot of anger over losing a year of my life. But what had I really lost? And more importantly, what had I gained?

As my long recovery came to an end, I finally made preparations to go abroad.

***

Experience in England

The travel bags were packed. I remember my stomach was full of nerves and my mind was spinning about living in Cambridge.

Tina hugged me goodbye and asked that we keep in touch as she left my room. We had been close friends since elementary school. I remember laying on my bed thinking about the past year and feeling proud of myself and thankful for my recovery. I couldn't help feeling like the next several years were going to be very challenging and rewarding. But it couldn't compare to the past year. It's strange to think how a major injury can change your life for the good.

My parents had balked at the idea initially. They did not want me to go to school overseas. But I craved a change, especially after a year of rehabilitation. That, along with my extensive reading, impelled me to Cambridge. I finally left, finding myself walking the same halls that Sir Isaac Newton and John Milton walked. Despite my accident, I joined the rowing team of my college. I loved the competition and being out on the beautiful River Cam.

Being away from familiar customs and culture wasn't easy. Bad food. The different sounds and spellings from my American English. At times, I felt like I had lost who I was, my identity, and my confidence. Lying in bed at night, I'd tell myself to stay positive. After all, this was an adventure. Keeping a daily personal journal and having new friends who kept me grounded helped my thoughts tremendously.

As I entered my third year, I realized getting an advanced business degree was not in my future. Business bored me then, and it bores me now. Through my volunteer work in the Cambridge hospital and remembering the great medical care I received after the accident, I decided to focus on the practice of medicine and return home for medical school. My parents were thrilled, and so were my Cambridge friends.

"Now we'll have a place to stay when we go the States," they said.

After I graduated, I spent six weeks touring Europe with two of my close chums. That fall I'd be on my way to Vanderbilt Medical School. After my acceptance there, I'd think of my grandmother, who wanted so desperately to be a doctor herself. Times were difficult (and different) back then because doors weren't open for women as much as they were for men. As a nurse, she was tough and dedicated to providing the best care possible for her patients, even if it meant confronting her senior male physicians.

As a volunteer back in high school, I walked into a patient's room where my grandmother was giving the physician a "piece of her mind" for delaying an order for the correct pain medicine. My memories of that formed my own standard for providing care and acting as an advocate for patients.

***

Enter Peter

Jog? Watch TV? Read a good book? I found out very quickly that in medical school there was no time for such distractions. Life revolves around classes, studying, and no sleep.

My classes at Vanderbilt were small so we all grew very close. It's kind of like when a group all goes through a traumatic experience together, they come out much closer in the end. Our trauma was medical school.

"We work hard, and we play hard" was our (not very original) motto. The "play hard" seemed more wish than reality, especially now. Money was tight. I shared a two-bedroom apartment with two other female classmates. I drove a 10-year-old Honda and avoided Nordstrom's like the plague.

Arianna, a classmate of mine from Mumbai, knew how to break away for play. It also didn't hurt that she was at the top of our class.

"Tonight!" she declared, "we're going to Tootsie's." (That's Tootsie's World Famous Orchid Lounge to you outsiders.)

"We've got a free night, so let's be free," she concluded.

Her brother, Hamid, came along that night. With him was his friend Peter from Chicago. The four of us drank and talked, which greased the wheels for Peter and I to continue once they'd left.

He told me he had graduated from Princeton and got his graduate degree at the University of Chicago, where he was on the faculty. I remember loving his sense of humor almost immediately, and his politics. We talked until after midnight.

"Can I call you?" he asks as we walk out.

"Sure," I said quickly. "That'd be great!" (I sounded so overeager.)

"Cool. I should be back in Nashville in a few months," he said, and smiled at me.

I soon realized how much I enjoyed Peter's company and wondered about a closer relationship. During that time he gave me space to be a medical student. He also supported me emotionally during some very stressful moments. It wasn't long before wedding plans emerged. It would be in my home church and a honeymoon in Italy. I just hoped I could get through school.

Peter continued living in Chicago while I worked as a resident at Harvard General. It was never ideal, but that was our reality for a while. He logged a lot of frequent flyer miles back then. When he wasn't flying to see me, we talked every night. We married after I finished my last month of my residency. Not long after, we started our new life in Atlanta.

***

Final Thoughts

As I drive home this evening from the emergency room, I reflect on my experience treating Robert. Life can be so fragile. I must never lose sight of my responsibility as a physician. In those moments, when a patient's life is on the line, I've got to stay focused on the treatment of the patient and leadership of my medical team.

"Please nudge me that you are safely home," says the note pinned to the message board in the kitchen.

I creep into each child's room and give them a kiss goodnight. In our bedroom I change into my black nightgown and slide carefully into bed, give Peter a light kiss on the cheek, and whisper, "I'm home."

The morning light comes much too quickly. Peter begins rubbing my neck and back.

"Good morning, sweetheart," he says.

"Good morning," I say, as I let him continue his massage.

We lie there, holding one another and chat about what has happened in our lives in the past 24 hours. I told him about Robert and the great teamwork of my staff.

"I'm very proud of you," he says.

We hear the children down the hall as they dress and head downstairs for breakfast. I enjoy spending this time with the kids.

"How's organic chemistry going?" I ask our high school senior.

"Not too bad. I've got a pretty good teacher," he says.

"Mom, are you and Dad going to be at my baseball game tomorrow?" Aiden, our ninth grader asks.

"Of course, honey. Wouldn't miss it," I said.

"Remember, Mom, you're supposed to bring snacks. And we're not little boys anymore, so bring things that will fill us up," Aiden says, as he darts out to Lorne's car for school.

A few minutes later, Peter arrives in the kitchen all dressed for work. He teaches U.S. and World History at Oglethorpe University.

"I love that tie. It's one of my favorites," I say as I hand him a cup of coffee.

"Glad to hear it. I mean, you did buy it," he says.

After Peter leaves, I put on my jogging clothes for my daily run, followed by 15 minutes of meditation and another 15 minutes of yoga. Then I write in my personal journal. This morning routine keeps me focused so I can manage my emotions, think positive thoughts, and be a good listener throughout the course of my day.

Arriving at the hospital, I check on Robert. He is in some pain but is comfortable overall.

"I'll be back after lunch to see how you're doing," I tell him.

He expresses his gratitude with a slight nod before closing his eyes.

On the second floor I step in to see the hospital's medical director to tell him about the great group that saved a patient's life. Dr. Anthony Philips thanks me.

"It didn't happen by accident, Karen. You hire the best talent here with similar values and the performance standards we expect at the hospital. You give them the best training opportunities and you recognize their achievements. That's why we have talented medical staff lining up to work for you. We're the best emergency medical unit in Atlanta and the region because of your leadership."

I'm overwhelmed by his words.

On my way back to the emergency room, I grab a cup of coffee at the Starbucks inside the hospital. At my desk, I think about my career, my family, and our future. My thoughts float back to my childhood and my college days. I was always focused on being the best I could be. I had great mentors from medical school to help me. How grateful I am to have a close-knit family supporting me every step of the way. How will I ever repay them?

***

The Future

Dr. West worked five more years at Grady Hospital and then joined a medical practice in Buckhead. She continues her daily routines of running, meditation, yoga, and keeping a personal journal. She manages her emotions, holds herself accountable, and demonstrates good interpersonal skills.

She cares about people. And that's what truly matters.

Reflection

1. Do I know people who have it "all together" like Dr. West? What can I learn from them?

2. Do I recognize people's accomplishments – small or big?

3. Am I a risk taker in my personal life and/or professional career?

4. Do I have a balance in my personal and professional life?

Chapter 5

Emily: Change is Hard

When a couple works as a team, great things can happen.

I am honored to have been chosen. I'll talk with my husband and kids about it tonight. I'm sure we'll all have a lot of questions to ask you later."

My law firm had just asked me to consider a position in London. They aren't sure for how long, but it'd be a minimum of three years.

"Please, take your time," my managing partner said. "We have a couple of weeks before we need to let the London people know."

My heart beats faster than normal, and my thoughts fill with excitement and anxiety as I walk back to my office. Sudden changes like this make me feel powerless, like I've lost control of my life. Yes, I know change is hard for most people, but it nearly immobilizes me.

This really could be a great opportunity to advance my career in the law firm. I could learn a lot about international monetary law and financial regulation, not to mention get the chance to work with our senior partners in Europe.

"Well, my favorite lawyer. What a pleasant surprise," my husband says, as he answers the phone.

"Adam, I've got some exciting news, but I'm going to explode with anxiety if I don't tell you. I know it's short notice, but can we talk about it before the boys get home from school?" I ask.

"Must be important. Sure, I can be home in 30 minutes. But, sweetheart, take a deep breath. Whatever it is, we can handle it," Adam says.

"Okay. Thanks, honey. I should be home soon."

Adam and I have been married for 10 years. We met on a blind date at the Kentucky Derby. His family raises Kentucky thoroughbreds. His family embraced me from day one, for which I have always been grateful.

We had only been married for six months before a large law firm in New York hired Adam. (He's mergers and acquisitions, and I'm employment.) That was a big change from our life in Nashville, to say the least. I made the adjustment slowly to life in Brooklyn, but encouragement from Adam and my older brother Thomas made the transition much easier.

My first thought upon returning to our condo is to pour some wine, but then I thought better of it. Wine tends to put me to sleep, I need to be fully present for this talk. There is a part of me that wants no major change in my life. The kids like their schools and friends, and our jobs are secure. Why change now?

Adam arrives, hugs me, looks into my eyes.

"So, what's up?" he says,

I lead him to the couch so we can sit face-to-face.

"I've been asked to consider a position in London starting in a few months. It would be a great career move, but I'm not sure it's worth disrupting your career and the boys' schooling," I say, nervously.

"First off, that's great, Emily! I'm very proud of you," he says, smiling and hugging me tighter. Adam seems to always see the cup half full. Mine's usually just plain-empty.

"We really need to consider if it would be worth moving the boys out of their schools and you from your position," I say.

"I'm not terribly worried about me. I can put in for a transfer to London or find something else there. The headhunters call every week. But this would obviously be a big change for the boys."

"I know. And they've been doing so well lately," I say.

"How long do you have to decide?" he asks.

"Three weeks," I say.

"Wow. They expect people to decide something like this that quick?" he asks.

"Well it does help weed out the ones not willing to make sacrifices."

We sit for a long while in silence, holding one another. Both of us are deep in thought as to what this change could bring, and if it is really worth uprooting our lives for.

Finally Adam speaks up.

"I think overall, this could be very good for all of us," he says.

"In what way?" I ask.

"Well, to make us all a little more well-rounded. In a worldly sense, I guess," he says.

"You know how much I hate change. This makes the move from Nashville look like a stroll across the street. I think we should consider everything before really deciding."

It took several days and a lot of discussion, but we finally made the decisions to move across the pond.

"I can't wait to see how the kids take it," he says.

***

Seven months later…

Adjusting to our life in London hasn't been easy. The excitement of what was initially an adventure has now become reality.

Working in the UK is not the same. There are entirely different expectations and workplace customs. For one thing, we get nearly six weeks a year of paid vacation!

The British value their privacy more than any other culture I've ever experienced. Conversations are shorter, and typically about the weather (which is almost always overcast and damp). People are friendly, but not outgoing. They're polite, but terse.

There are many cultural miscommunications. For instance, Pierce, one of my colleagues, was telling me about his son's rugby team. Throughout our conversation, I kept saying, "Oh, really?" In America that would typically translate to, "That's interesting, tell me more." But in London, Pierce thought I was questioning the veracity of what he was saying. Constantly. Finally he looked at me sternly and said, "Yes. Really."

Aside from the obvious differences in vocabulary, like "lorrie" for "truck" and "loo" for "bathroom," everything feels very trans-Atlantic. Similar with TV, movies, culture (sort of). It was just about settling in and getting comfortable, but that didn't come easily.

From the start, I noticed my confidence being shaken. I seem to want to second – guess all my decisions with work and the children's daily routines.

Adam, of course, handled it much better. He always does. Thankfully, he got the job transfer he had hoped for. He also seems to enjoy the challenge of new London office. He particularly likes his colleagues. The only true surprise to him has been the amount of travel. His work takes him all over Europe.

Adam and I have become closer. We share more of the house chores, including cooking and caring for the kids. Our talks are longer and much more intimate. We also enjoy planning weekend trips to neighboring countries.

We are more active in our synagogue than ever before. I must admit I was nervous about being Jewish in a European country, especially because there seems to be is more prejudice toward Jews here than in the States.

It had all been going so well.

Then one day a few weeks ago Eli came running into the house, holding his head and sobbing.

"Mom, it hurts!" he moaned.

I look up from my book and notice a bright red bruise on his right check, "What happened?" I say in a panicked voice. I knew he had been playing at the park down the street.

"No, two boys jumped on top of me and started hitting me."

"What! Why?" I ask.

"They called me a dirty Jew," Eli said wiping away his tears.

I pulled him into my arms and tried to comfort him.

Adam had an encouraging man-to-man with him later.

For the most part we are adjusting to our international life. They even enjoy the food. Their schools are first class with small numbers of kids in each class. One thing they miss is their television shows. But I must admit, I'm glad to see them go.

It is important to me that I fully embrace my life in London. I don't want to think and act like a tourist, either at work or at home. And I certainly don't one to let one vile (now that's a Briticism) encounter affect our whole outlook.

My fear of "change" occasionally creeps into my mind and heart rate, but I'm able to manage it by remembering how much support I have from my family and my colleagues.

Besides, three years in London might not be long enough.

We'll see.

Reflection

1. How do I handle change in my life?

2. Do I monitor my self–confidence?

3. Am I willing to take career risks?

Chapter 6

Kimberly: Marriage is Challenging

Lasting relationships require work, respect, and commitment.

My law practice can wait. The important things come first. Emma's kindergarten, for example. Her dance and piano lessons. Not to mention my son Matthew, also known as "The Handful," who is two years old. My kids always come first.

People ask if I've been working since I took time off for the kids. You bet I work. I'm a stay-at-home mom.

As another weekend approaches my thoughts turn lonely and boring, but no one will know. I'm good at hiding my unhappiness from my husband Doug. But it's getting worse. I am starting to feel a distance between us.

We've had open, honest discussions before, and they've helped. Early Saturday would be a good time so we could take advantage of the quiet while the kids sleep in. It's just about the only time we can have long conversations.

A few months ago, we tried to have a similar talk. We were on vacation. It was bad timing. It ended with both of us growing defensive, then angry. Then we walked away from each other.

Since then, I have thought a lot about my weaknesses. I've never been good at communicating my feelings. Even as a teenager, I was ultra-careful what I said around my friends. I've always held back my feelings.

Another problem I have is a never-ending need to please everyone. This can be a real burden. My mother pointed that out when I was just a little girl. I brought it to college. Even when I'm very upset with Doug, I still try not to show it. I am petrified that he will get angry.

Doug's not perfect either. For one thing, he wants to control everything about our lives – who our friends are, when and where we take vacations, even little family activities at home. Over the years, I've made mental excuses to avoid honest conversations about it. It's cliché, but it seems easier not to rock the boat. "Besides," I tell myself, "he'll get better."

I worry that he's grown bored with me. Our marriage is no different from anyone else's at this stage. We've had two children. We've moved to a new city. Both of us have changed jobs at least once. Early on, we were supportive of one another. He used to express his admiration for me when I practiced law, saying how proud he was, but I have not heard words like that in a long time. Maybe he's not as fond of me being a stay-at-home as he says he is.

I also worry that I am beginning to lose my appeal. Waning attraction is almost an inevitability in any marriage after a long enough time. I just didn't think it would happen this soon. I gained some weight after Matthew came, but now it's gone, and I'm in better shape than I was before the kids.

The alarm clock goes off, signifying another rushed morning in the Rumsfeld household.

"Doug, honey would you wake up Emma while I take Matthew downstairs and prepare breakfast?"

"Ok, but don't take long. I'm on a tight schedule this morning," he says, climbing onto his feet.

"Honey, one more thing. I'd like for us to have a conversation Saturday when the kids are sleeping in. You think we can pick up where we left off during vacation?" I ask.

"Can't. I have a tee-time at 10:00 with some of the guys from the office," he says.

"I want you to keep your tee-time. Can we just do it early? How about coffee –you and me – around 6:30? This is important to me."

"Ok, I guess. But it can't be long," he responds.

"Great! Can we agree not to get defensive this time?" I ask.

"Yeah," he says, leaving the room without a looking back.

Success in marriage is not a given. It requires work and commitment from each spouse. That's one thing I'm still in charge of: my own commitment. Meanwhile, Doug is running the rest of our lives.

I plan to get really honest with him. Tell him my true feelings, my needs. The truth. I owe him that much. And I owe myself.

As the week goes by, the distance between us seems to grow.

***

Arriving home that night, Doug enters the kitchen where Kimberly is feeding the kids.

"I've thought about it a lot," he says. "I suggest we start tonight after the kids go to sleep and continue in in the morning. You seem surprised?"

"No. I mean, good. Of course. I'll put the kids down early," I say.

"We'll split up their bedtimes," says Doug hugging her. "How about I read to Emma while you take care of The Handful?"

I'm encouraged by Doug's words and his affection. He even gave me a hug! It has been a long time since I felt warm all over like this. I don't want to lose this feeling.

We both sat down after the kids were in bed and talked for several hours.

"I spoke with Scott at work today," he started. "He said he and Jennifer had been going through the same thing we had."

"Oh," I said.

"I just had no idea how much of this was my fault. I guess I assumed that all marriages sort of hit a rut, and we'd just bounce back."

"Well, that's probably true. But it takes work to bounce back. It doesn't just happen, you know?" I asked as I put my arms around him.

"I had never thought about it before. I guess with the kids and work, our marriage got put on hold. I'm sorry," he said.

"It's okay. This is good. We can move on from here with a better knowledge of how to fix these things."

"When we were first married, I always enjoyed planning one or two date nights for us every month. When you started mothering full-time and left your law practice behind, I shared my work life and expressed how much I appreciated you delaying your own for the sake of our family. Now, I'm realizing I don't do that."

"It isn't just you," I said. "I've become complacent too. We both have to work to make things better. And I'd appreciate more sensitivity from you about how you want things."

"I know, I know. I isolate myself from the parental duties and 'bark out' how I want every little thing done. I'm not communicating with you on an emotional level like I once did. I'm a big boy. I know it's up to me how I interact with you."

"That's all I ask," I said.

"I love you."

"I love you, too."

Reflection

1. I'm aware of my strengths and weaknesses in my
2. relationship and will use them to attain a closer marriage.

3. Do I take the time to understand my partner's needs, feelings, and what we call issues?

4. Am I honest and open in my communication with my partner?

5. Can I pledge not to take my partner for granted?

Chapter 7

John: Heartbreak Hotel

Divorce is painful.

I haven't stayed in a motel like this since probably never. Now I remember why.

Sitting on the edge of the bed surveying the room, I make an inventory. On the ceiling I find two of those typically unexplainable brownish stains, plus cigarette burns in the duvet. There's an old television with bunny ears on the dresser. I would have stayed somewhere else, but this was the closest place. Plus I'm in the mood to wallow in my sadness.

"What a dump," I think.

Even through the hum of the old TV the room is quiet. I can feel my heart beating, echoing like footsteps in my head. I try to put myself anywhere but here. I imagine what it would be like to be lost in the desert or in some deep forest.

At least there I wouldn't have to sign any divorce papers.

Throughout this whole miserable process I've struggled to be honest with myself. I always come back to where things went wrong. They must have been a long time coming, but it's near impossible to trace them to the beginning now.

"What could I have done better?" I ask myself. "Was I really that self-centered? How much of this was my fault?"

She was just as much a part of the problem as I was, probably more. My defenses go up, blocking any real answer.

I have to be able to fight back the anger I feel toward her, no matter what has happened. I have to be in control of myself.

All I really know now is I'm emotionally hurting and feeling immense shame.

I remember back to when I first used to think life was tough. Managing the marriage, the kids, the career. Now I have a whole new set of worries. My kids may not even want to see me again. My ex could turn them against me, blaming me for this whole situation. In the state we are in currently, I wouldn't put it past her. Sooner or later the kids will see the truth, regardless of what she told them.

During this entire ordeal my family and friends have stuck by my side. I've heard all the clichés:

"It's not your fault."

"Just give it time. You'll find someone to love again."

"You didn't need her anyway."

While their words have been helpful, they can't get me back on my feet all by themselves. Only I can do that.

Constantly I remind myself that I'm a good person. I'm successful. I've been a good father and I've been very much involved with my two children's lives. I can be trusted and depended on.

I'm involved in my church and civic organizations. I coach my son's little league baseball team. I'm well-educated. I have been successful in two different careers.

There are many more good things to come.

But I won't fool myself, I've made many mistakes. That's something I've told myself I'm going to work on from here on out: reflecting on what I can do better.

At the end of the day, I most remember that I'm in control of myself, my thoughts, my emotions, and my life.

The sun will rise tomorrow!

Reflection

1. How honest am I regarding my strengths and weakness?

2. I must never take my marital relationship for granted. What are the behaviors that I must perform every day?

3. Do I spoil my spouse?

4. Can I have a respectful disagreement but also seek to have an agreement?

5. Do I tell my spouse five times every day I love her/him?

6. Am I a good listener when my spouse wants my attention?

7. Am I funny, caring, honest, respectful and loving toward my spouse every day?

Chapter 8

Ray: Retirement, A Love Story. (Again)

One effect of retirement is often falling in love again.

As the sun rises it begins to illuminate my backyard with color. Tiny raindrops glisten on rose petals, and birds chirp to greet the day. This my favorite time of the morning. All is quiet as I sit on my screened porch.

"Oops. Sorry, Patches," I say, almost stepping on my black lab as I head out to get the morning paper. I think I could get used to this morning routine. It's better than the 9 to 5 grind of speeding off each morning to work, fighting traffic, and the problems I was almost always faced with as soon as I arrived at the office.

"Ray, breakfast is ready," Aline calls out.

Patches and I turn in her direction. He runs ahead.

"Whoa, slow up there, buddy. You're not gonna eat before me," I say, brushing my hand across the scruff of his neck. It's my own fault, though. The old dog has been spoiled for the past 12 years.

For 45 years Aline and I have been side by side. Now that I'm retired, I need to get to know her again. I spent so many years working that I missed out on a lot of things, including a big part of raising our three sons. The reality is we haven't spent a lot of quality personal time together over those years. Now, it's time to change that.

I put the paper down so I can concentrate on her.

"How'd you like to go for a walk in a bit?" I ask.

"I'd love to," she says. "Once we finish breakfast, let's head down to the track."

***

Work has always been a large part of my life. Being raised on a farm you learn that it's as natural as eating or breathing. Of course as a young man, I whined about it. But one steely glare from my father always ended that quickly.

In high school, I worked at the local supermarket after school and on weekends. It was then that I realized the joy of having my own money. I could buy whatever I pleased. The money was all mine. My college years were no different, working part-time between classes from freshman to senior year.

Since then, I've been fortunate enough to have been employed my whole life. My drive, ambition, and work ethic always kept me in good standing with the boss. Promotions came easily. My career would eventually help put our boys through college.

Now, for the first time since I was 14 years old, I'm unemployed. I've been dreaming of this day. Being able to do whatever I wanted, whenever I wanted.

What I didn't anticipate was the boredom. It's nice not having a fixed schedule, but there are often times I miss the office. The hardest part is controlling that boredom. One day, I even found myself in a trance-like state scrolling through local bingo leagues. I shuddered at the thought of seeing myself end up like that.

My wife handles all this much better. She hasn't worked in several years, but she has learned how to keep her idle hands busy. I, on the other hand, am usually sitting in my chair reading the paper when she heads out each day.

"Where're you off to now?" I ask.

"Today's my women's caucus luncheon at city council. I told you that," she'll say. "

"Oh, right. Have a good time, sweetheart."

She's always involved in some class, shopping, or playing tennis. I feel like I just sit around. At this point, Patches and I are getting closer than I am with my wife.

Retirement was entirely my decision. I could've just kept on working through my 70s. I wasn't pushed out, my position wasn't removed, I wasn't fired, and the higher-ups were always pleased with my performance. I just decided it was time.

My dad worked seven days a week his whole career before starting to take it easy when he got into his 80s. It's relatively difficult to retire from your own farm. By that time, though, I had built up enough capital to help him by hiring some full-time hands to tend to the farm in his stead.

I was always told "retire at 65." I missed the mark by two years. I was lucky. My dad, not so much.

I suppose, in that sense, I'd better make the best of it.

If you've seen The Prisoner of Second Avenue. that's basically a documentary of what's happening to me. When the purpose of your life for over 40 years is a job, and one day that is gone, it makes you question your worth.

Today is Tuesday, and I'm on the couch again. The Price is Right is on TV. I stare at the screen listlessly. "Drew Carey doesn't hold a candle to Bob Barker," I think. My wife enters the room, pocketbook at the ready, poised to bound out the door.

"Hey! Where to?" I ask.

"Groceries, stopping by Big Lots for a sale, the usual routine," she replies.

"Um. Can I, uh, come along?" I ask, as I sit up.

Her expression changes from subtle surprise to a smile.

"Of course, honey. Let's go."

Driving to and from each store we talk. The conversation goes well. She opens up and tells me she's worried about how retirement is affecting me. I tell her my fears as well, and declare that I'm going to try and be as productive as possible.

"I can help," she says.

"Thanks, sweetheart. That means a lot."

In the next few hours I felt a small weight being lifted. Finally, I was beginning to accept my retirement. And it was because of Aline.

It was the last stage of my life cycle. Remember The Lion King and the circle of life? Well, like that, but with less singing, and no animals. Okay, bad analogy.

Two-thirds of my life had been spent at work. Now it'd be spent with the woman I loved.

Who would've thought that a simple trip to the grocery store would give me so much perspective? Before, I'd felt powerless. My purpose was gone, and I'd forgotten how to spend my time.

But I realized that I was in control of my feelings, I was in control of how I spent my time, and I was in control of my boredom. Bingo would have to wait.

I began reading books and magazine articles on the subject. I talked with my retired friends, my priest, Aline, and my children. Yes, I even talked to Patches, who either listened attentively or not at all.

I came to the conclusion that only I could be honest with myself about this question. There were many things in life out of my control, but I would simply focus on those that I could manage.

One conclusion was clear. I needed to spend more time getting to know my wife again. Our walks and shopping trips began to foster my gratitude for her. I was determined to make these the best years of my life.

But, I was admittedly nervous. I had never been an open or expressive person. I'm a good listener, but when it came time for me to share, I clam up. Just like at work, where I gave my best effort, I approached this goal of getting to know my life partner again with job-like determination.

***

Three months later…

Aline and I have found that the school track is a great place for us to walk, talk, and get in shape. We're out the door each morning after breakfast. Aline and I are new walkers and this is our first time making it a habit. So far, each of us has lost a little weight and gained some flexibility back in our arms and legs. We've also met other walkers, who are old neighbors. Some are new friends. But really, this is mostly our time to be alone and just talk.

I've learned again that my wife and I have a lot in common – a desire for European travel, a desire to volunteer, to make our community a better place, and the sheer pleasure of holding each other. I've known all these things about her, but I admit, I must have forgotten. I'd been too absorbed in my work and myself. What a wonderful experience to be around her and share with her the little things in life.

We also now know we want to visit the grandkids several times a year. In addition, Aline likes taking one or two of the grandkids each year to New York City, to visit the museums, and to see Broadway shows.

For me, I plan an annual golfing trip with our sons. We enjoy the long weekend, our talks, joking around with each other.

I've finally found that balance in my life that was lacking throughout my career. You always know intellectually that family is the most important thing in life, but we somehow forget. I'm just glad I realized it before it was too late.

***

Six months later…

My marriage is so much richer now. I think about how I could have been a better husband when we were raising a family and not too wrapped up in my work. It's not that I was an absent husband or father, but now I know the difference in the degree of my happiness. I'm determined to reach that new level right now.

We're sitting on the screened porch reading the paper, "Honey, can I interrupt you for a moment? I've got a poem I picked out to read for you."

"Of course, sweetheart!" she replies.

I clear my throat.

MY LOVE IS NO SECRET

When you enter the room my heart races
    My eyes zero in on you
    My feet land on the floor
    My back is straight
    My hands are sweaty
    My voice is gone
    My mind is full of happiness
    Suddenly, I wake from a deep sleep and turn over toward you and say…
    I'm thankful you lie next to me
    I'm thankful you love me so
    I'm thankful you said yes
    I'm thankful you are my life partner

    You look into my eyes
    I lean toward you
    We kiss and kiss and kiss

    She laughs. "Wordsworth! My favorite!" she says.

"No," I say. "I wrote it myself. Did you know?" Then I start to laugh.

"Well, first of all…" she says, giggling more.

I pause. Embarrassed.

"But you know what?" she says, as she puts her arms around me. "I absolutely loved it."

How did I ever wonder about what retirement would bring?

All along the answer was by my side.

Reflection

1. Are you finding times each day to notice your life partner? What can you do to make that relationship better?

2. How will you accomplish a better work/life balance?

3. Regardless of your age, are you thinking and planning for your future?

4. When life experiences are difficult, how do you respond?

Chapter 9

Mary: Love Will Trump Cancer

My religious faith and love for my spouse kept me going.

In a generic sort of way, I always figured something like this would happen. My 20-plus years as a registered nurse had given me some perspective about the brevity and fragility of life.

The early days of my career were spent working in the Intensive Care Units of major metropolitan hospitals. In that setting I came face to face with the kinds of catastrophic events that have the ability to shatter lives.

Sometimes our lives are altered in magical ways – childbirth, weddings, graduations – fabulous events that we dream about and plan for. In the ICU I was often witness to many moments when patients and their families were faced with the realization their future would be far different that anything they ever expected.

My last four years as a nurse were spent in the field of hospice where I specialized in the care of terminally ill patients who wanted to die peacefully at home. In that time, I paid close attention to patients and their family members to see how they were coping, managing, and dealing with reality.

Looking back, I think I was trying to prepare myself for the future.

Many times, as I watched a middle-aged woman cope with the ravaging effects of her own terminal illness, I would think to myself, "Now, when it's my time to go through all this, I want to do it with that kind of grace and dignity."

There were just as many times that I thought, "When it's my turn to go through this, I want to avoid the bitterness, anger, and hopelessness that I see in this person's life." That may sound judgmental, but everyone passes through this life in their own way.

I didn't find it difficult to apply either line of preparatory line of thinking to the possibility of me dying. I've never been afraid to die, so thinking about it doesn't cause me any distress. My faith and core belief in the promise of eternal life in heaven has certainly cushioned me from that fear. I am at peace with myself and accept my fate readily.

The fear of grief, however, is far more profound. The mere thought of my husband, or one of my children or grandchildren, or "seeing me die" has always made my heart tremble. And yet, I knew the possibility, even probability, existed.

Because of that, I've intentionally observed people moving through the process of saying goodbye to a loved one, and dealing with the aftermath of grief. I have watched closely, always hoping that I would never have to walk that path, but praying that if I did, I would do it well.

It should come as no surprise, then, that the very first thought that came to mind when the doctor told me that he'd "found a mass" in my husband's colon during a routine colonoscopy was, "So, now it's our turn." My second thought was, "I can't believe it's actually *our turn*."

Reality crashing into denial. Denial crashing into reality. At first there were copious tears, strangled breathing, elevated heart rates, and wordless, desperate prayers. But then, a very peculiar variety of peace began to settle in – sort of an unsettled calmness combined with an adrenaline-fueled empowerment, enveloped in a huge cloud of helplessness. These are contradictory words and even now, it seems impossible that so many conflicting emotions were infused into those first moments after hearing the news.

My mind and my heart instinctively reached out for supernatural strength. I knew that if my husband and I were going to get through this crisis, it would be with the help and guidance of God.

I was right about that. With God's help my husband and I did get through the initial days of crisis and more than a few crises since then. But the path hasn't always been clear, and our sense of control has been tested at every turn.

Learning to "expect the unexpected" is now a part of our lives. Each time something happens, I have to decide whether I'm going to rebel or submit. Sometimes I decide to rebel, and then circumstances require that I submit.

Do we submit to the "terminal" label applied to stage four metastatic colon cancer, or do we turn over every rock looking for the clinical trial that may be the key to a cure?

And how long should we go before recognizing that it's impossible to turn over every rock? How should we react if we find THE trial, but my husband is not accepted as a participant? What if I want to fight, but he wants to let go? Questions like these plague our lives every day.

My husband is a "go with the flow" kind of guy, so submission comes more easily to him. Chemotherapy is grueling, and it's easier to fight from the outside looking in. I think these have been some of most challenging moments: the times that I want to fight against this disease, and he either doesn't have the energy to join the battle, or he sees the futility of it. This is when I feel the loneliest and the most afraid. I have a deep desire to honor my husband's choices, but sometimes I wonder how I will survive if he dies.

Survival instinct is a powerful thing. I know that I'll continue to breathe if he dies, but that's not the issue. Continuing to breathe, you see, is part of the problem. What if I no longer want to? What if I find that I'll never be able to laugh, or have a moment's joy again? Can I really go on without him?

It's the memory of those who've come before me, my mentors, the ones I watched courageously navigate these treacherous waters that gets me back on track. I can almost hear them cheering me on, calling me to persevere, to press on.

There have been moments of respite in the years following my husband's diagnosis. For a time, we even thought he was cured. Initial surgery and long months of chemotherapy gave us a full year of normal life (if you can call it that), where the only remnants of cancer were regular trips to the oncologist for monitoring. I'm so grateful for that year. It was a special time that I will always cherish.

I've always heard that coming face to face with a life-threatening illness brings clarity to one's life, and it was true for me. Outwardly our lives didn't change. My husband continued to work with the same sense of purpose he'd always had, and my life continued to revolve around my church, my family, and my home.

We instinctively knew that our lives would be more intentional, more focused than they ever had been before.

Then, the recurrence of cancer came. We were all deeply distraught. Once again, we rallied and worked with doctors to establish a game plan.

The amount of support we received from family, friends, and our church was humbling, and I struggled to accept the help that was offered. I was overwhelmed with love. My independent nature rebelled, but I eventually submitted to offers of help as my emotional strength crumbled.

I desperately wanted to do something, anything that would make my husband feel better, or get better. I spent untold hours researching treatment options, medical centers, and clinical trials that I thought would change the outcome for him….and for me.

I bought a notebook and began to record the names and telephone numbers of people who said, "Call me if I can do anything." That notebook was a gift to myself, a way to take care of myself.

Encouragement came in many forms. Without a doubt, our church friends, and family, were huge sources of strength. Cards and letters arrived with the sweetest notes, and with Scripture verses that ministered to our weary souls.

I bought another notebook, and began to record every Scripture verse that someone sent to us – another gift to myself. It's a notebook that I pick up often, always feeling comforted by the words written in its pages.

Several years have passed since cancer recurred in my husband's body. He is no longer able to work, and it's becoming clear to us that the chemotherapy treatments will eventually be discontinued, either because they are no longer effective or because he can no longer tolerate the treatment.

So many transitions have taken place in the years since diagnosis: the transition from health to infirmity and from independence to dependence are the obvious ones, but there are many others.

It's interesting the way life can teach you to let go of long term goals, and set your hearts on the hope for a good day tomorrow.

I've been stunned by the way my heart can simultaneously contain grief and gratitude. I wouldn't have thought it was possible, but life has taught me otherwise.

The hardest part of being a caretaker has been watching my love, my soul mate struggle with disease and discomfort has been excruciating. And yet, we've been given the gift of time, and I've been given the opportunity to honor.

We've had the opportunity to say the things that we needed to say, and plan for the time that we'll be separated by death. I've drawn huge strength from the memory of many people who've walked this way before me with dignity, strength, love, and courage. I wouldn't say I've done it as well, but with God's help, I've done more than I thought I could.

Cancer can't win the battle in my husband's life, in our home, or in our heart. I think we made a choice, many years ago, that love would have the last word in our lives.

Reflection

1. What does this story to say to me?
2. Will I have the strength and faith to be such a caregiver?
3. Am I living each day as if it was my last day?

Section 2: *Work*

Chapter 10

Henry: Determined to Succeed

Two heads are better than one!

Nine months ago I graduated from Princeton. Today, I'm still living in my parent's basement. I've been trying to get my business off the ground ever since.

I'm still confident my software program can save physicians a lot of administrative time and streamline their fee collections. Both of my parents are physicians, so I've field-tested the software in their offices. And it works. This sucker is going to save medicine a lot of time and money in back bills.

The problem is that doctors aren't really lining up outside my basement door.

"Morning, Dad," I mumble, as I step into the kitchen. I'd been up all night thinking things over.

"Hey, bud. Any fish biting yet?"

"Well, I still have the first five clients. But no. None recently."

"Henry, I hate to say it, but do you think it might be time to get a real job? Not many kids your age have a double major from Princeton and no job," he says.

"I can't quit now," I say in a lowered voice as I go out to my car. "Not yet, anyway."

Driving to the Plaza Branch Library, otherwise known as my office, I started thinking about what my Dad said. Was he right? Is it time to give up the dream and get a real job?

I've never been one to give up easily. In high school I struggled to make the baseball and basketball teams, but by sophomore year, I was the starting first baseman and by junior year, the starting point guard.

My own parents tried to discourage me from taking on a double major at Princeton (economics and computer science), but I was determined. I graduated summa cum laude.

"Henry, you have no money, no friends, no personal relationships, and no job," I say to myself at a stoplight.

I'm not too fond of failure. When I know I've messed something up, I get this shortness of breath as my muscles begin to tighten. It's as if I have a physical repulsion to it.

As I sit down at one end of a long table, I slip my laptop from my briefcase. Before getting to work, I do a little Q and A with myself, an exercise which has always served me well.

Do I have the capital to continue my company? No. Do I have the guts and the willpower to put in the long hours needed? Yes. Is that enough? No. Should I try to sell my software? Yes. What will make this successful? Finding a buyer and making some money from the sale.

***

One year later...

A bitter cold wind swirls off of Lake Michigan. Still, life's not bad in the Lakeview section of Chicago, even at six degrees below zero. I hurry out the door of my building to catch the first a train and then a bus to my office. Public transportation and walking are the only real means of travel here. It's only eight miles to my Northern Trust office, but it's still a 50-minute commute – plenty of time to read the *Sun-Times* and yesterday's leftover *Wall Street Journal*. The four-block walk from the bus stop to my office gives me time to visit my favorite Turkish coffee shop.

Today's the day I learn if I've been chosen for a two-year Leadership Development Program. Like other things in my life, I was discouraged from applying because, according to the form, applicants have to be employed for two years. Plus, there were only 10 slots for an expected 50 applicants.

Even without the two years, I think I'm perfectly qualified for the position.

I know, I sound arrogant. Maybe even egotistical. But in this business you have to be, I think...

As an international stock analyst my success depends upon my attention to detail. If I'm being honest, reviewing data all day bores me. I need something with a little more variety. The program will give me two advantages: learning first-hand the different departments of the company and a choice of which business section to work in fulltime after graduation.

The phone is already ringing when I sit down to my desk.

"Hello, Henry. This is Mary Sloan in Human Resources. Could you be in the board conference room at 2:00pm today? You're to attend Mr. Carlson's announcement."

"Sure," I say. But what, I wonder, is the meeting about?

"Great! Thanks, Henry. Gotta run," she replies.

I'm too low on the totem pole to be invited to the CEO's meetings, so this could only mean one thing: I've proven everyone wrong again.

***

Two years later…

After 24 months in Leadership Development Program, I'm not surprised by my strengths – strong analytical skills, diligent, out-of-the-box thinker. My weaknesses aren't too surprising either: lack of good people skills and teamwork.

The thing is, I just don't like working with other people. I'd rather do things on my own, and not have to depend on someone else for help.

It's not that I don't like people. It's just I don't think I need them to be successful. Boy, was I wrong. All the higher-ups at Northern Trust have excellent people skills and rely on others for help. They lead more effectively and employees seem more engaged, more productive, and happier as a result.

I'm working hard to manage my ego and listen better. It's not easy. But the more I practice the behaviors outlined for me by the company's executive coach, the more I'm seeing positive results. Lately I've been receiving positive comments from my peers and managers in my department. I've still got a long way to go.

For the first time in my life, I realize how important it is to have good social skills. You really can't expect to go through life without some help from others. Learning this lesson will help me to someday become a better leader, and a better person in general.

***

Four Years Later…

Leaving Northern Trust was not easy. My family and friends thought I was too young and a bit too cocky to have left such a great job to start my own company. But all I could think about is having my own company again, only this time it'll be different. This time, however, I won't go it alone. I will surround myself with talented people.

With a bit of luck and some help from my expanding professional network, I have an idea for a high tech healthcare company to be located in Austin, Texas. Healthcare is an industry I know all too well from my years in that department.

Now to assemble my team.

My first choice is one of my closest (okay, one of my few) friends from Princeton. How anybody could get bored in New Orleans I'm not sure, but Bart Kerrigan has done it.

A lawyer by trade, Bart proved his worth becoming a senior associate in just a year at his firm. He's as dedicated as I am to his burgeoning career, but I think I can convince him to take a chance with me.

"Bart, how'd you like to be the COO of a new healthcare company? It's going to take a lot of hard work and long hours, but we'll be in control of our hopefully successful futures." Three months later, he signed on.

Bart's a good role model for me. He works well with people and knows when to listen, to encourage, or to motivate staff. And most importantly, he's not afraid to give me constructive feedback.

Next on the call list is another Princetonian.

Anne McIntosh is one of those Mad Men ad wizzes. Originally a creative writer, she shifted her focus to marketing and has worked in creative departments for some of the biggest companies in America. Always freelance, Anne is never in one place for longer than the job at hand.

"Hello?" Anne says.

"Hey, Anne. It's Henry," I say. "Listen, I need your help promoting this new company of mine."

I then went on to explain everything to her. How our work would help the healthcare industry, what direction and tone I wanted to establish in the industry, and how much I truly needed her. It wasn't easy for her to leave her free-wheeling life, but she was finally convinced once she realized the importance of my product.

With Anne and Bart ready to go, it was time for my third call – to the No. 1 person on my life list. We've been talking ever since we met on a beach in Cancun three years ago – she in broken English, me in busted Spanish. Somehow between our two languages we became special to each other. Pretty soon there'll be an old-fashioned Catholic wedding in Monterey.

***

Five years later…

I have a full schedule today, but the early morning basketball pick-up games at the club keep me level-headed. My YPO (Young President Organization) buddies and I rarely lose. Of course it helps that all of us are over 6'1" tall, and none of us like to lose.

Raising my son William is my newest, and probably most difficult job yet. Honesty, respect of others, accountability, hard work – these are all character traits I hope to pass along to him.

The work of overhauling myself never stops – it's even more important now that William is in my life. Over the years I have learned that it's important to be constantly self-aware. I strive to know to some degree the direct result of my words and actions, and to examine and re-examine them if things go differently than I expected. This awareness allows me to better manage my thoughts, feelings, and behavior. I also make it a practice each year to get formal (and confidential) feedback from my staff. Keeping a personal journal and meditating daily helps tremendously as well.

It's been a long road from "I'm the best, I know everything," to deferential leader of a team with similar values and a determination to help change the healthcare industry.

I'm a different person now. I'm having fun watching employees work as a great team. It's not all about me. It's about all of us. That's what spells success for us.

Today we'll be receiving a new temporary member to our team. A young man interning for the summer. His résumé is strikingly similar to what mine was at his age. Similar grades, clubs, extra-curricular activities, and ambition.

"Joshua is here," my assistant says over the intercom.

"Great," I say. "Send him in."

I watch as my door opens slowly, and a young man, tall and slender, walks in. He stares at me for a moment, scratching his arm nervously.

"Hi, I'm Joshua," he says timidly as he extends his hand. "I really appreciate this opportunity."

"Of course. And it's nice to meet you as well, Joshua," I say. "Walk with me."

I lead him out into the main office where our team is. I want everyone to hear what I have to say to him.

"Joshua, we're excited to have you spend your summer here. You'll be learning from all of us and you'll also be learning a lot about yourself. You'll be challenged and tested, and sometimes your job may seem impossible. The most important thing is for you to develop in your time here is an awareness of how your actions impact others."

He looks to me, nodding.

"Trust me," I tell him. "I learned the hard way."

Reflection

1. How is your self-confidence? Is it over-the-top or realistic? Has it ever hindered your performance in work or in other areas of life?

2. Do you hold yourself accountable for your actions?

3. Would you say you have good social behaviors?

4. Where do your strengths and weaknesses lie in social situations?

5. When you have doubts about yourself, what do you do to remove those doubts?

Chapter 11

Thomas: I Must Lead

At times, we struggle with, "I'll do it myself. I don't need you."

I have always struggled with the board of trustees. They ask too many questions about all of my recommendations and want me to "hold their hands" between meetings. They take too much of my time. They know too little about what it means to run an institution.

Then, of course, there is the faculty. They live in a world of their own. I seem to have these same thoughts over and over as I jog through the streets of Washington, D.C. every morning.

I still have a lot to learn as a college president. After 18 months, I have finally realized my role is leading, not managing; it is listening, not telling. It is about creating a vision, a mission, and core values for the college, not just about tending to daily details, though there are plenty of those.

"It's getting a little wintry," I tell my wife Marie as I step into our enclosed back porch from my run.

"I'm not ready for winter," she says quietly.

"Well, it's coming."

Thoughts about my crowded calendar accompany me to the shower. I see a mental picture of it, with all the days nearly blacked out with activities. It seems I spend all my time on campus in meetings with no breaks in between.

I miss my time as dean. I really miss being a classroom teacher. It was both fun and fulfilling to read up and prepare my lectures, conduct research, and, best of all, spend time with my students. Now I spend time solving rather large problems and asking for money. Maybe I'll adjust to the change sooner than I think.

A short walk from our house takes me to the shops and stores near campus. I enjoy the energy of the city and the movement of people racing to work. Like every college denizen, I have my favorite coffee shop.

"Good morning, Tina. The usual, please." She smiles and begins making my drink.

"Dr. Snider?"

I whip around to see a tall gentlemen with a briefcase approach me. Uh oh. It's a professor.

"Do you have a minute?" he asks.

I love conversing with my faculty as much as the next president, but I know all too well what this will be about.

"Bartley Donovan. I'm with the Russian language department."
"Good to see you, Professor Donovan," I say as I shake his hand, silently wishing I had skipped the coffee this morning?

He gets right to the point. "Is it true you're going to cut Russian and Polish?"

Before I can respond, Professor. Donovan swings into full rant.

"I just want you to know that would be terrible for the present students and would send the wrong message to potential students and faculty. Couldn't something else be cut? Maybe something from the athletic department?

By now, his hand has sharpened into a single pointed finger aimed at my chest. Before I realize it, my eyes have narrowed and my body has gone stiff. I respond rather forcefully:

"Professor Donovan, I appreciate your concern and your obvious passion for our university. I would, however, suggest leaving the financial matters of the college to me. We are always looking to provide the best, most well-rounded education for all our students. Programs without enough students may get cut. If you'd like to inspire more students to take classes such as Russian or Polish, we may be able to bring them back at our year-end review. It is entirely up to students and faculty to determine that. And despite your personal feelings about athletics, it is a strong sports program that pays for more niche studies such as the two you named. I certainly thank you for your comments, though."

I feel the eyes of other people in the coffee shop on us. He makes a slight grunt as he brushes past me, and my outstretched hand, out the door. All is silent. I look over at Tina, get my coffee, and leave. My heart was beating out of my chest. I maybe shouldn't have been so hard on him. I felt cornered. Is it bad that I love proving people like him wrong, though? His intentions were pure, but he hasn't a clue what it takes to run a university.

As I walk on, my mind races to a number of other issues – the future role of liberal arts, e-learning courses and degrees, fundraising, increased enrollment, binge drinking, and date rape. A college campus is really a city within another city. We have similar financial, social, and infrastructural challenges. And at times, I certainly feel like a mayor instead of a CEO. My thoughts stop as I enter the city hall, I mean the administration building.

I'm admittedly concerned about my cabinet meeting this morning. Several issues have arisen because two of my vice presidents have failed to address them. These are two intelligent and experienced individuals, but they haven't made the needed changes. I may need to intervene, but I hate having to clean up other people's messes. They won't like that much either.

I feel like I have to do everyone else's job. It's just like the old adage, "If you want something done right, you better do it yourself." This has been a problem with me since group projects in grade school. I always volunteered to lead. Then I would end up writing the report for each team member to review and approve. The paper would get an A+, and my teammates would get a "free ride."

Fifteen minutes before my cabinet meeting, I look over my agenda and my notes.

"Be a leader, not a micromanager!" I remind myself as I enter the room.

For once the cabinet meeting is a success, and we were able to come to an agreement on administrative cuts, benefits packages, etc. Things this group would normally never come to a consensus on.

"Looking forward to sitting down with you this afternoon," I say to Audrey Price, the VP of Academic Affairs, as I leave the meeting.

"Me too, Thomas," she replies.

I breathe a sigh of relief as I enter my office. My few moments of solitude end abruptly as Ms. Rodgers enters.

"Dr. Snider, here are the files you requested. You're meeting Mrs. Brown, Chairperson of the Board of Trustees, at the Faculty Club at noon."

The future of some liberal arts courses is going to be a sensitive subject over lunch. My board is inclined to keep things the same. If we could, my job would be much easier.

The truth is, we need talented business and academic members. People who know how to plan, make tough decisions, raise money, and set high standards. That's the only way to create a vision and establish the core values of students, faculty, and staff.

Over the past six months Mrs. Brown and I have visited every board member.

"Are you committed to the necessary changes we are facing and the new trustee responsibilities?" we asked all of them.

Not surprisingly, some members immediately chose to resign effective end of academic year. Now our challenge is to find strong successors.

The Faculty Club is a nice walk from my office. I start early, hoping to visit with a student along the way. They really are great kids, and I love to hear about their home life, how they spend their spare time, their travels, their families, and their friends. I always ask: "Do you have any recommendations for me?"

In front of the library, a young man greets me.

"President Snider? Do you have time to answer a question?" he asks.

"Of course. At least, I'm happy to try."

"My name is Levi Knight, I'm a junior." We shake hands.

"Where're you from, Levi?"

"Duluth, right outside Atlanta."

"Of course, I know Duluth. What's your major?"

"Currently pre-med. Though I feel like I may switch," he says nervously.

He laughs nervously.

"What can I help you with?" I ask.

"I wanted to speak to you because I think students would learn more from each other if we were actually in class. A lot of students ask smart questions and make insightful statements that add to the professor's lecture. So why are we given a choice between attending class and downloading our professors' lectures? Everybody ought to be in class."

"The truth is I don't know why," I say, running my fingers through my hair. "It's become standard practice at most colleges, and we don't want to appear out of step. It was adopted originally for students who couldn't make the commute to and from school. I guess it's sort of been abused, hasn't it?"

"Yeah. A lot of students get away with never attending class because of it."

"Thanks for letting me know, Levi."

There wasn't really an easy solution for this one. Good or bad, we made that decision and it would be hard to change back to the requirement that students must be in class. Of course, the class faculty member can require it.

I arrive at the Faculty Club with 15 minutes to spare, enough time for me to gather my thoughts before my meeting with Sara.

Hearing Sara out – really listening to her – will help me to understand her view of the major issues that the board needs to address. I have done plenty of research on the necessity to change Liberal Arts, but I had better move much slower than I want.

"Good Afternoon, Sara. Thanks for taking the time to meet with me," I say as I rise from my chair to greet her. "I've been looking forward to our discussion."

Two hours pass. I'm surprised at how closely I've been listening.

"Thomas, Liberal Arts is the foundation of this institution," she says.

"Well, Sara, change isn't easy. As we plan for some changes, we will retain our legacy, our traditions, and the high academic standards we uphold. The bottom-line is our major donors over the next 10 years want to see such changes, that is provided we don't sacrifice our values. My goal is to walk the thin line between the new vision of a liberal arts education and the traditional one. "

Here's a good example of what I hope we will see more of. For the past two years one of our professors, Professor Hing in the Engineering Department, and several of his freshman and sophomore students have been involved in helping villages in Nigeria have access to clean drinking water. This is a huge problem in most remote villages, as they cannot afford to purchase the needed purification equipment. So Professor Hing challenged his engineer students to design and create the equipment needed for these villages.

Most college students are like these students. They just want opportunities to improve the world. They welcome the challenge to explore outside the classroom.

As we shake hands to depart, I tell her, "Thank you again for your insights and suggestions."

"Of course," she says and waves goodbye.

I think back on my meetings with key faculty members in the last few weeks. Jacob Lee from Psychology is a godsend, though he does get a little salty at times. He agreed to chair my faculty advisory committee with a caveat.

"I'm not a kiss-ass. I will serve if the discussion is about the quality of teaching, the research we do, and what's best for our students. No political side trips," he told me.

"You're on, Jacob. That is my agenda too."

The advisory committee meets monthly over lunch in my boardroom. Our faculty is superb. They teach more than their counterparts and they do vigorous research. "Gladly would they learn and gladly teach," to paraphrase Chaucer. They have also learned the fine art of increasing grant proposals – a 25 percent increase.

A 15-minute meditation at the office breaks up the day. I'm trying to get better about my self-awareness and self-control which helps me to be a better listener.

My daily are appointments over, so I burn through some emails, return a few phone calls, and prepare tomorrow's agenda. My wife and I have a reception at the Cosmos Club at 7:00 pm. I am very fortunate to have a "working partner" as my wife.

I met Marie in graduate school at Boston College. She grew up in Puerto Rico in a family of nine. Being an only child, I came to enjoy my time with her large family. Our four children keep us very busy. Marie has a unique way of combining household management and supporting a college president.

"Sweetheart, you look wonderful," I say as I kiss her. "Tonight will be a lot of fun. The Russells will be there and so will Diana."

Marie smiles, "I am looking forward to seeing them. And I've got my talking points ready about the new business school library. Oh, and Kate will be keeping the kids tonight. She says she can come whenever we need her." "Great! Kate knows how to handle the kids' differences. Growing up as the children of a college president and seeing your father castigated on Twitter is not fun for your children."

"Uh oh," she says. "What's next?"

Marie is better at working donors than I am. When I attend fundraisers, I notice my heartbeat increases and my hands get moist.

I'm working on this by remembering that fundraising is an important part of my job. Besides, Marie loves it and serves as a good role model.

At the club, a surprise visitor: Professor Donovan.

"Good evening, President and Mrs. Snider. Bartley Donovan," he says as he extends his hand. "I would like to introduce my wife Julia."

"It is a pleasure meeting you, Mrs. Donovan, and running into you again, Professor." I should have been in more control of my emotions during our disagreement. When Marie and Julia step over toward the waiter offering white or red wine. I take the opportunity to apologize.

"Professor Donovan, please accept my apology for my behavior this morning in the coffee shop. You have every reason to ask about the future of the Russian Department and the athletic budget. I would like to invite you and other members of your department for a lunch discussion to hear your concerns. And please call me Thomas."

"No need for an apology. You made some valid points that I hadn't considered. I would love the opportunity for my colleagues and I discuss our concerns," he says.

Marie arrives with a glass of red wine and says, "Ok, no more business talk, we want to get to know you," as she smiles at Professor Donovan.

"It's going to be a great evening," I thought, smiling.

It's quiet as Marie and I return home and relax in our bedroom. *The Iron Lady* is ready to be read, but before turning the pages I thank Marie for a wonderful evening and being such a good brand for the college. We kiss, and she turns over to sleep.

Before I give my attention to Margaret Thatcher's life story, I reflect and write in my personal journal what I noticed about myself today:

"During several conversations, I noticed I talked too much and talked over the person speaking. At times my thoughts would stray off the person's subject and I would struggle to refocus on the subject. I also recall only once that I let my emotions get the best of me."

For me to be an inspiring college president and leader people want to follow, I must learn to be in control of myself.

Reflection

1. What really triggered Dr. Snider's anger in the coffee shop?

2. Is it hard for you to delegate to others?

3. Do you use some form of meditation?

4. Do you feel as though you are in control of your thoughts, feelings, and emotions?

Chapter 12

Allison: Single is Not Simple

The freedom of being single has both pros and cons!

It was Amy talking. Again.

"You're so lucky, Allison. It must be so nice to go home and not have to worry about taking care of children. You just don't know how hard it is juggling the job, the husband, and the kids. You must have so much free time. I am so jealous."

I listened quietly as Amy invoked a familiar theme. I was trying desperately not to show my irritation.

It's typical. Amy, like so many others, assumes that anyone single and childless has no obligations outside of work and nothing to do in their spare time but shop and drink wine. If only that were true.

I always find myself in conversations with people like her. Asking about their husband or their kids was always a good conversation starter. I couldn't care less about how little Jimmy got runner-up at the science fair, though. When they finally get to asking about me, if they're even polite enough to do that between their kid's soccer practice or piano lessons, it usually goes something like this:

"So… How's, uh, your dog?" they'll say, brightening up with pride as if remembering I had a dog was some great accomplishment.

"Pretty good," I reply. "Just doing dog things."

What could you possibly say about a dog? "Well, she threw up on the carpet yesterday, but I got it cleaned up. Then she slept for a few hours."

"Well that's good," they reply.

And then we stand there for a few more seconds, before they go, "Well, see ya around."

I'm 34 years old, single, never married, and yes, there are no children in my life. I am constantly told how "lucky" I am. Or reminded that "the one" will come along soon when I least expect it. Give me a break.

I am the middle child of three. My siblings are both married, with sweet kids. My parents will celebrate their 48th anniversary this year.

As the only single child, I often find myself treated *like a child*. I sit at the kid's table at some holiday gatherings and often end up with babysitting duties. But I have a lot going on in my adult life that none of these people even consider. Like yesterday for instance.

I woke up at 5:00 am because I had an early meeting, I immediately noticed something wasn't right. My face was cold and so was the hardwood under my feet. The heat pump had failed. Just what I needed.

I called the service company, got the after-hours line, and reported my problem.

"We'll have a technician call you to set up a time to come by," the woman on the phone said.

How am I going to fit this into my day?

Then I kicked off my morning routine: walked the dog, showered, made breakfast, packed the trunk with dirty laundry, grabbed my coat, computer bag, lunch, and purse. I also had to run to my landlord's to drop off rent, not normally part of my routine.

Pulling out of the garage, I remember I need to leave the key for the housekeeper. So I stopped, hopped out, ran back inside to get the extra key, and put it in its hiding place. It always makes me happy to come home to a clean house.

Surprisingly I arrived at the office on time and ready for my client meeting at 8:00am. I was excited to take second chair for this trial.

The senior partner is Robert Dunn. Late 50s, married for half that, bear of a man. Four grown children, two of whom now attend Ivy League schools. He's all business and has little sympathy for personal matters. When I arrived at Magnus and Robinson a few years ago, I was excited to learn from a lawyer like him.

I thought I might have a nurturing boss who would help me grow personally and professionally. Very soon, the truth emerged. Where Robert Dunn is concerned, you were on your own.

On one very rare occasion, I was 15 minutes late. It was because I had to run to the bank for a new debit card. Mine had been reported for fraudulent charges and had to be cancelled. When I approached Mr. Dunn in his office, I tried to explain the situation. As I was talking, he did not look up once, just continued working. When I paused for just a moment, without lifting his head, he pointed to the door. In utter disbelief I slowly turned around and walked out. This was two months into the job. An hour went by and I received an email from him, no subject line, that simply read, "Don't let it happen again."

All of this meant there was going to be no leaving the meeting to talk to the service tech. I prayed they wouldn't call until after the meeting was over.

We ran long. Just as we were saying goodbye to the client my phone vibrated, and I took the call. Luckily the technician was able to schedule a time to come by the house this afternoon after a deposition was over.

Crisis averted. Or so I thought.

I went to Mr. Dunn's office for debrief. His first remark was that I should have been more professional seeing the client off. Leaving without a formal goodbye was not acceptable to him. I then explained the urgency of the call.

"Couldn't that wait?" he responded.

Sure, I thought, easy for you. Your wife probably handles all domestic issues, and probably without you even knowing. It just gets fixed. I apologized, though, and we continued our meeting. I left his office frustrated but with no time to dwell on it.

My phone vibrated again.

"Dinner Friday?" the text said. It was from Rick.

I've known Rick since my second semester of law school. At the time he was a first year associate, and I was clerking at his firm. We had an immediate connection. He and I have a lot in common, including a searing love-hate relationship with the practice of law.

We've been out twice recently for last-minute drinks, but I don't hear from him regularly. This is the first time he's asked me out in advance. Needless to say, I was excited.

Fridays are the worst, though. I am always exhausted, and just want to decompress after the long week. But I couldn't say no. My mother always said, "If you say no too many times, people will stop asking."

Okay, Mom. I'll go, I think to myself, feeling oddly like a child again.

Rick has many redeeming qualities as well: upwardly mobile, friendly, socially adept, and most important, kind. Being a lawyer as well, we're able to really relate to each other about the demands of the job. On paper it's a perfect relationship.

I text him back saying Friday would be great, silently sending up a prayer that I won't be too tired. Sometimes I enjoy the freedom of being single. I work. I travel. I do what I want, and I answer to no one.

But the loneliness can become hard to overcome at times. Having a relationship, while challenging, would be so nice.

Back at my desk, I took a minute to relax. Not soon after my assistant, Carol, charged into the room.

"Remember, you have that brief to write and one of the partners is already asking about it.

"Thanks, Carol. I get on it," I said. I immediately pulled it out, and continued through lunch as I ate at my desk.

At 1:00pm I got in my car and drove an hour to a neighboring town for the deposition. En route, I was able to make a couple of client calls, and then break off to think for the last 20 minutes of the drive. I am trying hard to be at least 15 percent above my minimum billable hours for the year. Working at home through dinner and right up until bedtime is the norm. Thankfully, the deposition started on time and was relatively straightforward.

Afterward, I began the trek home. Hope the ole house hasn't iced over, I thought. I had never planned to be this stressed on a regular basis. I always knew I wanted to be a lawyer, but the truth is, I didn't really understand what that meant. I was not prepared for the work hours, the office politics, the competition, and the lack of hands-on training.

It has slowly driven me crazy. I still love so much about the work, though. It's intellectually stimulating, the clients are interesting (sometimes), and as strange as it sounds, I get a real rush from litigation that you just have to experience to understand.

I had hoped the service call would be quick, but the motor had apparently died and needed to be replaced. The tech said he would be back tomorrow to replace it. He recommended I get a space heater for the night.

It was 5:45pm and once again I would never get to the cleaners on time. I've been trying to get this laundry to the cleaners for a week. Why is it that every cleaners closes at 6:00 pm? Don't they realize who their primary clientele is? What a terrible business plan. Before taking Daisy on her evening walk, I sat down to catch up on email.

I was happy – and stressed – to find an email from the managing partner, Bob Magnus. He wanted me to take on a file for him (always good news!). and he needed me to entertain a potential new associate on Friday evening. So much for date night.

The new case could be a big opportunity. The more work is from the boss, the more upward movement.

Bob's request to entertain a new associate is just one of many I get mostly because married associates and those with children are often relieved of that duty. I don't want to disappoint, but what about Rick?

In a rare moment of bravery I email Bob that I will gladly work on the new case, but tell him I can't make the dinner with the new associate because I have a conflict. I felt myself shaking with adrenaline. I've not once turned down anyone at the office, much less a partner.

Then the old doubts kicked in. Bosses don't like being told no. I also didn't want another associate to take out a new candidate either. Oh well, I'll just have to show my commitment to the firm through my work.

I walked Daisy, then made a quick run to Wal-Mart for a space heater, calling my mother on the way. It feels like being in the car is the only time I'm able to make calls to friends and family. Usually by the end of the workday I am so tired of talking on the phone I don't want to punch in another number.

She told me that my Uncle Dan had just been diagnosed with lung cancer. The prognosis is worrisome. After hanging up with mom, I immediately called Uncle Dan and Aunt Lucy to talk with them. It was difficult. These are two of my favorite people. Their sadness makes me sad. Thank God they have one another.

As I talked with them I prepared dinner. When they were 34, they had been married for years and had two kids. Flash forward to me at the same age: eating a Lean Cuisine at 9:30pm with my dog and a stack of papers to read.

No one is here to share my news. I can always call friends, but it's too late tonight and I hate to burden others. Instead, I took some time to read today's devotional and make my gratitude list. That usually helps. Looking through my list, I am reminded that I'm healthy, safe, secure, and have options. I guess I couldn't ask for much more.

Thanks to my new space heater I could actually feel my toes when I woke up. Daisy sleeping by my side didn't hurt either. I did my usual again – dog, shower, breakfast, and today, I even took extra time to do a morning devotional. It always feels good to have that extra time. It's something I should do every morning.

Driving to the office, I ran through my assignment checklist: finish brief, report on deposition, start work on new file for Bob, get heat pump fixed, drop off laundry and maybe most importantly, make time to get ready for dinner with Rick.

I felt confident that I could do all this today. And I was excited that I finally had something to look forward to (a rarity these days).

I arrived at the office and headed to the kitchen for a cup of coffee. There I encountered Amy. Amy is 40, a partner, married to an insurance broker, and the mother of two kids under five. She informed me that she is "stuck" taking the new associate to dinner. Thankfully she doesn't know it was me who passed this off.

I was relieved that she was doing it and not another associate, but I felt silly for being so competitive. She tried to play it off as a joke, but there are no truer word said than in jest. Other than Robert, most everyone in an office atmosphere is constantly hedging. They're sizing you up. Light comments like, "Left a little early yesterday, didn't you?" or "That took a while to finish," really mean "Stay later," and "work faster."

"Come on, Allison, wouldn't it be more fun for you to go out with the new associate? I don't know the single lifestyle. You go out all the time and know the cool places. You can show her a good time."

"I really can't, Amy. I already made plans for tonight. Think of this as your first night out in a while, away from the kids and your husband," I said with a nudge. She sort of laughed, thank God.

"Also, I never go out anyway," I explained.

"Sure you do," she said, a quizzical look on her face. "You've got to be out all the time with the freedom you have."

"No, I really don't. I'm usually trying to catch up on work, or run errands that I couldn't get to during the week."

Amy rolled her eyes.

"My caseload also doubled recently. It's been kind of a rough week," I concluded.

"You don't know how lucky you are," she said.

I felt silly for confiding in her. I had believed that as one of the few women in the firm she would be someone I could talk to. She just couldn't see how someone like me could have serious problems too.

It just seems like my life is somehow less important or valid because I'm single. I really don't know if these people even remember what it was like. Does marriage cause some kind of amnesia?

I went back to my office and closed the door. I finished the brief and got started on the file for Robert. At lunch I went home and let the repairman in to fix the heat pump. Thankfully, I would have heat when I got home.

Back at the office, I shut myself in again. I finished without interruption. Leaving at 4:45, I actually made it to the cleaners on time. Thank God for small favors.

As I drove I grew increasingly distracted by the thought of isolation – personally and professionally. Is it time to explore another career track? Thirty more years of this is enough to drive anyone insane.

Then I remembered the date with Rick and smiled. Maybe things wouldn't be so bad after all. I headed back home, crossed my fingers, said a prayer, and hoped that things would be simpler tomorrow.

Reflection

1. Do you think single professionals have it more or less difficult than their married counterparts?

2. Should Allison have chosen Rick over the associate dinner?

3. Do you think Allison is starting to take more control of her life? Or will she fall back into the same old habits?

4. Has Allison taken control of her personal life?

Chapter 13

Philip: Millennial Mishaps

This generation is different, but wasn't every new generation different?

It my last Christmas break before I graduate from Fordham University, and I'm wondering what the future holds. I've got to get a job, that's for sure, and that job has got to pay me enough to start knocking down these student loans. Worry is not what I want to bring home for the holidays.

Christmas Holiday

Charleston is so great at Christmas – the lights, traditions and the air in the Lowcountry are like nowhere else when winter arrives. We've got a big house, and it's going to be filled with family – aunts, uncles and cousins.

Everybody's gone home. Nobody lives more than a couple of hours away so they bail out after a celebration that starts on the afternoon of Christmas Eve and finishes with Low Country Boil at lunch on Christmas Day. For a week they were part of our lives morning, noon, and night. Now, gone. My dad and I are sitting out on our porch, taking in the dying light over Charleston Harbor. I look over at him; he has a thin, contented smile on his face.

"Dad, how can I get a job," I ask, sipping a bourbon and ginger.

"That's the big question, isn't it?"

"Yes, sir, it is," I say, looking down at my Docksiders.

"It's no easy task, but with some luck and some focus, you'll get a job.

Your first job is typically never the one you want, but everybody ought to have one lousy job in life. You'll do fine in the long run, that's for sure."

"I guess you're right. I'm a little worried, though. If I'm being completely honest."

Dad hesitates for a minute, taking a sip from his Madras.

"I think I may know of someone who can help. I'll make some calls," he says, smiling. He puts his arm around my shoulder and gives it a squeeze. "We have five or six months, maybe even longer. You can do a lot in that amount of time." Then he adds with a grin: "Maybe you can do some work around here too."

Soon after packing up my things and heading back to Fordham for my final semester, my Dad found me a career consultant to help ease my mind and hopefully increase my chances of finding a job.

Her name is Sharon Sutlive.

"Good morning Ms. Sutlive. It's a pleasure to meet you." I say. We're skyping one another. "I reviewed the checklist you sent. I can't wait to get started."

"Good morning Philip, I look forward to working with you. If you're ready to get started, I am too."

"Definitely," I say, a little startled by her directness.

"Now, about your resume. I have a few suggestions. The key to landing a job is standing out from the crowd. At this point you're just another number, a faceless, 20-something. Major companies receive thousands of resumes a week, most of which look just like the draft you sent me. Yours has to have something that will grab their attention."

"I see." I look down a bit nervously at my own resume.

"Another essential is a good cover letter. Each cover letter should be tailored for the specific job you're applying for, but the general text you can go ahead and draft."

"Okay, I'll do that," I say, pulling out my phone to Google "cover letter" whatever that is. "Thanks, Ms. Sutlive."

"Don't worry, your resume will be fine. It's a lot better than some of the other millennials' I see. Most young adults I work with these just expect to be handed everything with little or no effort."

"Yeah, they worked us pretty hard in English at Fordham. Too bad for anybody who didn't go through *that* ring of fire. You're right, though. My generation sort of grew up thinking if we just got good grades, went to college, and graduated, we'd get jobs just like y'all did. That hasn't really happened."

"Trust me, I know the statistics, and you're right. But with a little help, you won't become another statistic. We're going to get you that job."

The Hunt Begins

For the next several months I constantly edited and changed my resume. I wrote five different cover letters (it's apparently exactly what it sounds like, a letter that acts as the cover of some other pages) – one each for different positions. Ms. Sutlive and I held several mock interviews where she would grill me on a variety of questions, some of which we had practiced and a few she made up on the spot. It was brutal at times, but by the end, I felt I was ready.

Graduation came and went. I held on to my strong GPA, graduating with honors. I moved back to my parents' place and set up in the basement. The job of finding a job had begun.

Weeks went by. Every day I was on Indeed, Monster, you name it. I applied for positions way out of my league. I applied for everything. I applied at the Gap, and I hate shopping.

Nothing happened. Not even a form letter. Every entry level job that I might've qualified for bore the caveat "two years' experience." How the hell do I get experience to get an entry level job when I can't land an entry level job to get experience? The logic of that was enough to drive me nuts.

I started to unwind. I began waking up later and later. I spend my mornings playing video games, or drinking by the pool with my fellow unemployed. My dad began to notice.

"How's the job search coming?" he'd say, three to twelves times a week.

"Really good," I replied, closing the Facebook window and changing it to the Monster one that I kept open for just such occasions.

"Any responses?"

"Yeah, I think I might have something with this IT recruiting firm outside Atlanta," I lied.

"Great," he said. "Keep it up."

As he walked out of the room I flipped the browser back to Facebook. I sighed and got up from my computer.

"There has to be a better way of doing this," I thought. "I'm going about this all wrong."

I only had two friends who got jobs right out of college. My friend Derrick found a job selling fiber-optic cable for a tech company. And my friend Andrew was hired as an accountant for a medical software company.

They never told me of how they landed these jobs, so I finally asked. To my surprise their stories were strikingly similar. Derrick got his sales job from a friend of his dad's, a neighbor. The neighbor was retiring and the company was looking to fill a position. The neighbor put in a good word, and the rest was history.

Andrew got his job because his mom was in medical sales. She knew the VP of the company he now works for.

So my only two employed friends really had nothing to do with the jobs they got. They just had to graduate and show up. Grim reality began to set in. It really is who you know, or these days, who your parents are. For as much help as Ms. Sutlive had been, I hadn't prepared for this. That night at dinner I figured I'd come clean.

We were sitting around the table, everyone enjoying our red snapper. My dad finally looked up. He must have sensed something was wrong.

"Everything okay, bud?" he asked.

"Yeah, it's fine," I said.

"You sure?" he said, looking across the table at my mother. She shrugged.

"Well, actually, I'm starting to get worried about this job search."

"I thought you said you just got a response? That's progress, right?"

"I lied. I haven't gotten any. I just didn't want to disappoint you."

I went on to tell them about my two successful, job-holding friends. I explained that they had really just gotten the jobs because of their parents.

"You should have come to me if you needed more help," he said. "I have a few connections."

"I know, but you'd already hired Ms. Sutlive. And I wanted to do this on my own."

"Son, no one gets a job on their own, especially these days. You almost always need to create a strong network – someone, who knows someone, who knows someone I'll see who I can get in touch with tomorrow. We'll figure this out."

I sighed, knowing what would happen. My dad would call one of his corporate buddies to explore possible people to contact. I had wanted to do this myself, but here I stood.

A few months later I ended up with a job at The Coca-Cola Company in Atlanta. I'm what they call a marketing assistant. It's not bad.

I've come to realize that millennials aren't the lazy, self-obsessed, "want everything handed to them" generation everyone has been led to believe.

We are passionate about our work, social issues, and having close friends.

We are an ambitious group of young people who want to love what we do.

We want to work hard and be given the opportunity to do so.

Many of us, when the job search failed, have created our own jobs. This is one of the reasons so many millennials become entrepreneurs.

We are grateful to all the generations that came before us, and we promise to not let you down. Yes, we believe in having fun, but we are also confident, talented, hard-working, and truly want to help others.

Were you much different at my age?

Reflection

1. Have you ever helped a young adult get a job?

2. Do you demonstrate self-confidence?

3. Are you open minded to the Millennial Generation?

Chapter 14

Sarah: Work and Family, Where Do I Say No?

The balance of work and family is hard for me.

"Absolutely."

That's what I told my boss, Jack, when he asked me to take over the company's strategic planning process.

Jack trusts me. He believes I "can get the job done and done right," which is great. His compliments seem to be getting old, though. It appears sometimes the only reward for good work around here is more work.

Don't misunderstand. I love my job and want to stay here and advance as far as possible. I'm very focused on achieving my goals. Not to mention goals other set for me. In general, I feel challenged, affirmed, and appropriately rewarded. To remain relevant and important I always answer, "Absolutely."

From Jack's office, I headed straight into my next meeting. That's how my days go. Meetings every minute. Many left you feeling that, "There goes another hour of my life I'll never get back" kind of feeling.

It was a lot of talk until somebody asked the question.

"Who's going to put together the next proposal?"

No one raised their hand except me. I have done it before and know how to make sure it is done right. There I go again, sounding like

Jack. This new job is going to affect some of my other ones. The new product development, for example.

A launch in three months will now take six, which means I'll be doing twice the paperwork.

But there's no time to think about that. I have to get to my next meeting.

Why did I have to sound so enthusiastic to the boss when I agreed to take on this new job? What was he thinking? What was I thinking? Shouldn't I stay in my lane?

The third meeting of the day was a nice reward. Kelly had some solid ideas on improving the product development pipeline, and it was an awesome session. Kelly is new and doesn't have the experience to be the lead on this idea, so I will have to lead that charge, too.

The change should be implemented in six weeks. Naturally, this pipeline development conflicts precisely with the new product launch. I hope Kelly is ready to become a key player around here.

One thing I miss most about my days in midlevel management is lunch. I used to take full advantage of the midday break and get totally away from the office, get some space, try for a new perspective, and then come back energized for the afternoon. Not anymore. My lunch hour is now filled with personal appointments and community commitments.

Today my big appointment was with the doctor. We got to find out the sex of the baby. My husband, Paul, met me in the waiting room. We met with the doctor for the ultrasound, had a quick snack in the car, and were back at our offices in under an hour.

Sometimes I marvel at my own ability to schedule the joy right out of life. The baby, I should mention, is a girl. Alice and Elizabeth will be so thrilled to get another sister.

I am a little bit of a reluctant mother this time. When Paul and I got married I was 33 and he was 37 and we both had careers in full swing. I assumed that we would not have time for multiple children, let alone one child.

Neither of us felt strongly about it when we started out. I was probably closer to a total kiddie ban than he was, but I wasn't opposed. Now I am 40 and pregnant with my third child in four years. What were we thinking? Now the children will outnumber us. Even a full night's sleep is only a dream these days.

My assistant, Corey, called me on my way back to the office.

"What's up?" I asked as I answered the phone.

"Your 1:30 appointment has been delayed," he said.

I had just been given 15 minutes.

I used that time to call Brian in marketing and discuss our joint presentation to the board of directors on the latest product launch.

"How's it coming?" I asked as I tried not to sound demanding.

"Pretty good," he said. "Things are moving right along.

He was always vague like that, but I really was so grateful that he agreed to do the first draft. I just hoped he would have that finished by the end of business today.

The rest of the day was spent in a team meeting with two new associates. Walter has extensive industry experience and should be able to hit the ground running. Caroline is only two years out of college and will require a lot of guidance.

The rest of my team of 10 are all men, so I feel it's important that I mentor Caroline myself. I figured I'd start having coffee with her once a week before work to guide her along. I look back to the women who helped me and those who were roadblocks; it's my obligation to be the former in my office.

I always wonder if thoughts like these cross the minds of the male managers in my office. There will always be some other man to mentor the young guy starting out. Men are still the majority around here.

The team meeting ran until 5:00pm and was very productive, despite the fact that the team continues to depend on me too much for direction. Some of these guys have been at this company for years and in the business even longer. Is this my fault? It's hard to tell them to figure something out themselves when I can contribute.

I now have 45 minutes before I have to leave to get home by 6:00. Thankfully, Paul picks up the girls from daycare and starts the evening routine without me. This last 45 minutes of the work day goes to emails, which can reach over 80 a day. There are five phone messages, and some urgent in the inbox on my desk. But at least the office is quiet.

I drive home in silence, still pondering the new projects and all the work on my plate – mentally planning the next day, the next week, the next month. My cell phone rings.

It's Bill from the staff of homeless shelter where I'm on the board of directors.

"There was an incident this afternoon," he says.

"Uh oh. What happened?"

"For the third time this month someone tried to steal the communal laptop," he says. "They're calling an emergency meeting to address it. Can you be at the shelter tomorrow at 8:00am?"

As I drive, I pull up my schedule, and figure that I can cut my mentoring coffee with Caroline short and move my 8:00 am meeting.

"Yeah, I can do that," I say.

Bill hangs up, and I call Corey, who (bless her heart) always answers. I ask her to rework tomorrow morning so I can be at the shelter from 8 to 9:30. She sounds unhappy with me, but how could I say no? I feel awful for bothering her at home but I've gotten far past letting those feelings stop me. Still, without her help I'd be drowning.

Home at 6:00pm and, as usual, it's a zoo. Paul does his best. He's a litigator and he's tired at the end of the day, too. Toys and coloring books and markers are strewn about the floor. The girls sit moonfaced on the couch watching SpongeBob. I have to put on my "Happy Mama" face and prepare for my next starring role.

Paul was starting dinner. When I arrive we take a few minutes for all of us to talk about the new baby sister arriving. Everyone's excited and they all come up to my belly and say hi to No. 3. In that moment I am reminded what a blessing these babies are.

I take over the kitchen as Paul disappears upstairs for some pre-meal quiet time. After dinner we watch TV and play. We get both of the girls bathed by 8:00pm, and in bed at 8:30pm. Paul's on story duty tonight. For maybe the eighth straight night it's *Where the Wild Things*

Are. I loved the book as a child too, but if I hear about the "wild rumpus" one more time, I may scream.

Afterwards, while talking for a few minutes about our day, I tell him about the strategic planning project.

"It'll be a lot of work. But I can handle it," I say.

"Are you sure?" he asks. "On top of everything else going on? You're spread a little thin, honey. And this is coming from a lawyer."

He looks at me sullenly. Paul knows me and he knows that I'm "all in" on everything. Now, on top of my 70 hours a week, my family, and my pregnancy, I have taken on this huge company-wide project.

"I can handle it," I say. "Just got to segment my time is all."

"If you say so," he replies.

He acts as though he can't believe it. But he's not totally surprised.

I want to talk through Paul's frustration, but by 9:45 I have to get back to work – what some might call the third shift. Tonight I'll review Byron's draft presentation for the shareholder meeting.

The final draft is due on the president's desk in two days. I try really hard to be asleep by midnight. I go to bed around 1:00 a.m., though. The revisions are more significant than I'd anticipated. I'm going to meet with Byron tomorrow about his choice of content when talking to the shareholders.

I can't sleep. Getting up to collect my thoughts, I find I can't focus because of my guilt about agreeing to take on this project has intensified. Once again, I didn't stop to think about putting work ahead of my family.

Paul's frustration is legitimate. I should have taken time to think about it. I should have talked with him first. Pleasing my husband and family means more than pleasing my boss.

I'd hoped a good night's sleep would make me feel better about the new commitment. Look how good I am. Forget that. Look how exhausted I am! Look how bad I feel about myself as a wife and parent. The disagreement with Paul has me thinking about my priorities and why I feel the need to please people at work and not so much at home.

I leave the house at 6:30 a.m. with a throbbing headache. Paul gets the girls to school and daycare on the days when I have 7:00 a.m. meetings.

Coffee with Caroline is my only respite lately. She's bright, funny, and willing to work. I often tell her what a wise friend once told me: "Be careful when making work your life and life your work." I feel insincere as the words fall out of my mouth, knowing that my life probably seems like a cautionary tale to her – two kids and one on the way, a successful career, and a husband I rarely spend quality time with.

Everyone on my team knows it, but it seems like they're holding back. Again, the reward for good work seems to be just more work, but with that work comes more money and with more money comes an easier life.

I wonder if men feel like this. Paul doesn't seem to, even though he is driven and competitive. Though he's a partner at the firm, meaning he has lots of control over his workload.

Maybe I'm the victim of a triple standard. Good mom. Good wife. Good manager. But all of those things at the same time is near impossible.

The homeless shelter meeting is less painful than I thought it would be. Luckily, the board is quite cohesive and we have what is basically a public relations and media problem under control.

Back at the office at around 9:15, I get a panicked call from Paul. Daycare says Elizabeth is sick – projectile vomiting sick. He is starting a trial in the afternoon and can't leave the case.

This is the moment when I wished we had just sucked it up and hired a nanny. Then I immediately feel guilty for thinking that. I love my girls, but I can't leave the office because I have a meeting with the president and an important customer at 10:00am. I just can't miss it.

We agree to call my mother for Elizabeth and then I will work from home this afternoon. We are both irritated as we hang up. I call Corey to reschedule my afternoon and then my mother to pick up Elizabeth. Thankfully, she is happy to do it. Another crisis averted.

I find a quiet place to gather my thoughts before going to see my boss and a new customer. I'm good at burying my feeling of frustration about my life choices. In a few minutes, my confidence is restored. I'm ready to go in.

My boss spent the first 10 minutes of our meeting telling our customer what a great asset I am to the company. He mentions my agreement to lead strategic planning.

Maybe this isn't so bad after all. I'm on the right track at work; the approval and confidence of the boss are solidified. Maybe this news will help Paul feel better about it. I'm doing the right thing for the future of my family and the company. It may be hard, but it is a win-win.

Or maybe I'm in denial.

Paul's trial runs until 5:30, so Elizabeth (sans vomit) and I pick up Alice from school. I'm able to do my last phone conference of the day from the car. Luckily the girls are quiet as they watch the latest Disney movie from the back seat.

I am pleased with myself. I have the girls bathed and fed by 6:00 when Paul gets home. I try to get ahead with my work while the girls play. Maybe I'll get to bed earlier tonight. I only have 55 emails to return.

The trial isn't going well, Paul tells me as we eat dinner. I listen carefully. I thought that my news of the boss's enthusiastic affirmation would improve his mood. I was wrong.

We spend the next four hours arguing off and on, between getting the girls through their bedtime stories and then to bed. Once again, the topic is my workload and my willingness to take on new projects. I never thought I'd have to clear a work project with my husband. At the same time, I see his point and deep down feel he is right.

"Paul, I just don't know how to juggle all of this right now. I recognize my decision was impulsive and selfish. I'm sorry, but I can't undo it. It would tank my reputation. I mean, what kind of message would it send to my team?" I plead.

"I can't do any more to help our situation either. However, a question for you: what kind of example are you setting for our girls, Sarah? What the hell are your priorities?" he asks.

"Goodnight, Paul, I can't deal with this right now. We'll talk tomorrow."

I turned away from him and closed my eyes. I went to bed feeling guilty and sad.

Reflection

1. Are you able to say no?

2. Do you struggle with work-life balanced? If so, why? What can you do to change?

3. Does your family really come first?

4. Do you identify with Sarah? Have you lost control of yourself through work?

Chapter 15

Gene: Will I Make the Right Decision?

Making personal and professional decisions determine the many pathways of our life.

"Wake up, Gene. You overslept," DeAnna says, as she opens the bedroom curtains.

"Okay," I mumble, as my feet hit the floor.

It's an important day. Mark Kaufmann, our CEO, wants to see me. I can't imagine what he could want that requires me at his downtown office this early. Usually, we'd just talk for a few minutes. The work is stacking up on my desk as it is.

The kids are leaving for school by the time I am finally dressed and ready.

"Study hard," I say.

I don't worry about our oldest, Walter. He's adjusted to middle school well. John has been having a little trouble and he's only in the fifth grade. DeAnna and I need to arrange a parent-teacher conference. I just need to find the time.

During the drive to Mark's office, the radio stays off. No phone calls. No texting. I need complete silence.

A lot of possibilities are running through my mind. Does he want me to handle a business deal? Probably not, because he would have called me and then sent over the information. I'm praying he doesn't send me to some boring corporate conference in Chicago or make me join a community board. He is always nagging me to go on a bunch of boards.

I get there right on time and head to the elevators. The door opens to the 50th floor and I proceed to Mark's office, still unsure of why I'm here. I give several staff members a half-smile that says: "No conversation, please." Judy greets me and immediately calls Mark.

"Mr. Kaufmann, Mr. Roberts is here."

Seconds later, Mark swings open the door, "Great to see you, Gene. Come right in."

Mark's office has a beautiful view of the Mississippi River. I walk toward the window to look at the steamboats and tankers moving along the mighty stream. Mark sits down in his ebony leather chair. I take a place on his deeply cushioned gray couch. He has an almost annoyingly comfortable office. Pictures and little chachkies line his desk. The only thing missing is a Zen garden. Nonetheless, my conversations with Mark over the past eight years have been short and always straight to the point. They're mostly about growing our commercial loans, the latest regulatory issues, next week's management meetings, so on and so forth.

"Would you like a cup of coffee or some water? I'm going to ask Judy for some," Mark asks.

Mark has always been pleasant in conversations and is a good listener. That doesn't stop my heart from racing, though.

"Sure," I say in a soft voice. It occurs to me, I'm sitting here with nothing in my hand. It feels strange, how do I carry on a business conversation with no agenda and paperwork? I set my hands in my lap for a moment, then fidget and place them on the arm rest of the couch. Then back to my lap.

"How's the family?" he asks.

"Doing great," I say, caught off guard with a personal question.

"Good to hear," he says.

Judy walks in with the water.

As she walks back out, Mark smiles and begins to open his mouth. Uh oh. Here it comes.

"Gene, I'll get right to the point. I want you to transfer here, and take the president's slot. I'll stay on as CEO but focus more on business development, partnerships, and stakeholder relationships here in St. Louis. I need a person like you who knows the business of banking and has a solid reputation in the industry. I realize you have some hang-ups regarding your people skills, but that can be fixed once you put your mind to it. What do you say?"

"Mark, I'm at a loss." My hands are already sweaty.

"Gene, I understand completely," he says.

"I really wasn't expecting this. I'm going to need to think about it."

Mark looks shocked. What else could I say? I like my current job. I don't want a new one.

"I thought you'd be more excited," he says. "But I understand, you need some time. I'll need to know your answer within the next day or so."

"Thanks, Mark. I really appreciate the opportunity. I'll give you a call tomorrow."

Leaving the office, I avoid eye contact with Judy, slipping by her desk, and Tim in the hallway as I walk briskly to the elevators. My mind is spinning.

Did I really hear the word "president?" A regional bank president is a demanding job – major visibility in the community, the burden of retaining key customers, and always demonstrating strong leadership. I just don't know if I have it in me. Besides, Mark is right about my people skills.

I've always just avoided interactions with customers. I'm not particularly shy and I don't lack self-confidence, I just don't want to bothered. My brothers and I were taught respect for others, as well as the obligation to serve others. My mother even used family and church settings to teach us people skills – instructing us before we got somewhere and then giving feedback afterwards. Only now do I realize their true value.

Over time my social skills just became less important to me, giving way to my desire to work hard and meet my goals. I've always been a bit of an introvert. Even social settings nowadays cause me to withdraw to a quiet corner and spend time with only one or two people. After being with people all day, I need time to recharge, to get a few hours of alone time each day to really remain socially adept. That, unfortunately, is proving harder and harder to come by. I'll have to strike a good balance if I am to take on this new position.

Walking up the stairs to my office on the fifth floor, I groan at the thought of so many financial reports to review. I must hurry to my office.

"Good morning, Mike," Bob says, swinging in alongside of me. "Some of us were just talking about *Jersey Boys*. Have you had a chance to see it yet?"

"No I haven't," I say. (I should have walked faster, I thought.)

I sit down to the pile of loan applications on my desk. As soon as I begin to gain momentum, I'm interrupted.

Patrick, a junior commercial loan officer, knocks on my door, opening it before I had a chance to say, "Come in."

"Sir, do you have some time to discuss the Hoover application? This loan app looks pretty good," he says.

"Patrick, are you kidding me?" I say in a gruff voice. "Spend more time with the numbers and with their ownership. You're easy to fool. Come back tomorrow when you're more knowledgeable about the numbers and their business plan." I point to the door. He closes it hurriedly.

Nancy enters my office with telephone messages, "Mr. Roberts, here are some of your messages. Several more are on your voicemail. Lindsey dropped by and wants to see you. I told her I would check with you and call her back."

"For now no messages, telephone calls, or people. I am going home," I say.

"Yes, sir. Oh, how was your meeting with Mr. Kauffman?"

"Fine," I say softly.

On the way home, B.B. King accompanies my 30-minute commute. I return to two fundamental questions. Why me and why now?

During my banking career, I've never thought about being an executive. My mind returns to my days in business school at the University of Iowa. My fraternity brother, David, talked a lot about being a CEO of a large corporation. Me, I just wanted to work for a good company like my Dad's. He had a State Farm Insurance agency. Now that I think about it, I never aspired to be a banker. It just sort of happened. I'm not entirely sure what I want to do with my life personally and professionally. I've never seriously thought about it. One minute I was graduating college, and the next I had two kids and a career. It's strange waking up one day and feeling like you've been just a passive observer of the events in your life.

My days are spent going from one meeting to another, completing tasks and playing the role of father and husband. I snap out of deep thought in my driveway, and I'm not sure how long I've been there. I hope DeAnna is home.

I could really use her advice.

She's in the backyard tending to her flower garden. Hearing my footsteps, she turns around.

"Hey!" she says. "I'm so glad you're home early." She gives me a long, warm hug.

"Mark wants me to be bank president," I blurt out. DeAnna pulls away.

"What did you say? Start at the beginning."

"There is no beginning, honey, just a bottom-line. I'm not sure I even want to accept. I like my job, and I absolutely do not want to go to all those corporate meetings in Chicago."

My voice grows emphatic, almost parade-ground loud.

DeAnna knows to stay calm when I become agitated.

"I'm very proud of you," she says as she looks me deeply in the eyes. "You've worked very hard. You deserve this."

There is a short silence before she continues, "You'll be a great president – I just know it. And Mark knows it."

I wish I did.

DeAnna takes my hand. "Well, since you're home, you can take Walter to the batting cages," she says with a nudge. "I have to pick up John. He had to stay after school again."

"Okay," I say with a shrug. She always knows how to bring be back down to Earth. "How long is practice?"

"Just an hour," DeAnna says.

I give her a small peck on the cheek, an unspoken thank you for talking me through this. Most people who aren't married don't really see or understand these unspoken conversations, but after you've been with someone for so long, it becomes a second language.

Driving to the baseball field, I'm quiet. Thinking again. Doesn't it make perfect sense to be promoted? What is mentally holding me back?

I realized my son is in the car with me.

"How was school today, buddy?" I ask.

"It was good. I really like my history class. I have an A so far."

"That's great. Keep up the good work," I respond.

Walter mature for his age. He performs well in school and sports. It was his idea to get a batting coach.

In the indoor facility I introduce myself to his coach, Roger. He has quite a grip. Full of energy.

"Gene, it's been a pleasure working with your son. He takes practice seriously and learns fast," he says.

"Today we're going to work on the balance of your back foot as you swing," he tells Walter. Walter walks over to home plate.

I take a seat behind the screen and watch. I begin to think about this process of receiving instructions, performing the requested action, and getting feedback on it. It occurs to me that I have never really received feedback about my people skills.

The weight of my decision sits heavily on my shoulders. Why would I change my life at the bank? I'm comfortable, and I'm good at what I do. Heck, my future plans might be about moving to Denver or Santa Fe before the kids start high school.

For the past seven years, Mark has really been an outstanding leader both in the bank and St. Louis community. I don't want to disappoint him. He was the one who gave me the opportunity to work at the bank in the first place. He taught me about the trade and promoted me to senior commercial officer. He has supported me when others in the corporate office would not approve my loan recommendations. He's even sought my advice, on occasion. Sometimes he just wants to talk about various issues in the industry. I never realized he wanted me as his president. I've been blind to my working relationship with Mark.

"Hey, if Mark thinks I can do the job, then I will make it happen!" I say to myself. "I'll just have to work on my weak points. Practice is over."

"I've decided to take the position," I tell DeAnna as I walk in the house.

DeAnna is delighted. "Gene, you'll make a great president!" DeAnna has more confidence in me than I have in myself. Thank God I have her in my corner.

Once the kids have finished their schoolwork and climbed into bed I decide it's time for the call. I can't wait any longer.

"Honey, I'm going to call Mark now," I tell DeAnna as she begins reading a book in her favorite chair.

Just tell him, I say to myself.

Mark answers his cell phone.

"Hello," he says in a strong and confident tone of voice.

"Good evening Mark, I couldn't wait till tomorrow. I accept your offer. I appreciate this opportunity and will not let you down. DeAnna is delighted as well."

"Outstanding," Mark says. "You'll do a great job, Gene. Can you come by the office sometime tomorrow to discuss the details? We'll work up your compensation and discuss starting date."

"Sure, I'll call Judy in the morning. Mark, listen. I really appreciate you putting your faith in me. No one's quite stuck up for me the way you have. I really am at a loss."

"Gene. If you saw in yourself what I see, you'd have wanted the position years ago. No one is born with charisma. No one is born with the ability to talk through any situation. It has to be instilled in you. We all have a perception of ourselves and how others supposedly perceive us. While you have a few social hang ups, you are incredibly focused, and graceful under pressure. You're going to be great, and I'll be there to help along the way."

I stand with the phone in my hand, staggering. I'm speechless. Quite literally, because the next thing I hear is Mark saying, "Thank you. We'll talk tomorrow. Good night, and congratulations."

The next morning I call Judy, and she arranges a lunch meeting with Mark. Then I gaze out the office window smiling to myself.

"I've made the right move. I'm in control of my future," I think.

Then something occurs to me. There's a junior commercial loan officer who needs an apology.

Reflection

1. Do I have the right amount of knowledge and skills to perform above average in my current position?

2. How are my people skills? Do I manage my emotions? Am I a good listener? When was the last time I asked for feedback regarding my people skills?

3. Leadership is not about one's position in an organization or amount of money a person has – it is about leading, inspiring people for the "good of the whole." Effective leaders are needed in all levels of an organization. It's time for me to get started on building my leadership behaviors.

4. Gene thinks he can change himself to have good people skills. Can he? Can you?

5. Am I in control of my thoughts, feelings and strong emotions?

Chapter 16

Joe: Is It Ethical?

My mother always challenged me to "do the right thing."

I can't wait to start my new job. I'll finally be off the road and into an office. For the past two years, I've been traveling. Don't get me wrong, there were good parts of traveling for work, and I made plenty of money. But I missed my wife, Miranda, and son, Bryan, at home, waiting for me, and I really missed them. Anyway it's a win-win – I get to go back to the work I love and spend more time with my family.

Human Resources is my vocation, it requires consistency and integrity. I believe I have both of those virtues.

Most people have an irrational dislike of HR professionals. We're considered the hall monitors of the corporate world, the tattletales. This couldn't be further from the truth. People consider us corporate spies, when really, we're there for their benefit. We serve the employee just as much as we serve the company. Straddling that line is what turns a good HR professional into a great one.

***

For the last three years I've held my position as HR vice president. My work is rewarding, but it can also be very frustrating and difficult in many ways, too. I'm reminded of this as I sit in the executive conference room.

In a wingback chair, facing Lauren's back, I have one hand on the arm of the chair and the other holding a paperweight on the side table. It's heavy, made of glass.

"What would happen if I threw this at the back of her head?" I think to myself. I answer my own question: "I would feel better, but only for a moment."

I can't stand to be in the same room with Lauren Carson. Her presence infuriates me. It's irrational, I know, but I'm overwhelmed. This is how things have gotten.

Lauren is smart, attractive, and well-educated. She is also a lying, cheating manipulator who uses others to get what she wants. The saying applies: "She's like Teflon, because nothing sticks."

Lauren is the Vice President of Finance. We both report to the president. Luckily, I don't have to report to her.

I do have to work *with* her, though. And I am nearing the end of my rope, with her and with my boss. The staffing issue at hand directly concerns my department. The issue: would my new employee, Sam, be exempt or non-exempt?

It shouldn't have even been a point of discussion. Sam was filling an entry-level position and didn't meet any of the legal requirements for an exempt employee. It's fairly obvious. Yet, there we were, wasting valuable time discussing it.

Salary level was not the only qualifier, I pointed out. The employee had to have a certain level of autonomy and decision-making authority. That was not the case with Sam. As I was speaking, I could tell Larry, our president, was getting frustrated with me. I was not telling him what he wanted to hear.

"Joe," he said. "Wouldn't Sam qualify if worked over the 40 hour a week minimum?"

"That would possibly get him to the level he needed for qualification. But only as long as we paid him overtime in accordance with the law," I replied. I should have been surprised by Larry's next comment, but I wasn't. It's the kind of thing I deal with every day.

"What are the penalties for non-compliance?" my boss asks. "How would someone even find out?"

Lauren chimed in: "I mean, it doesn't seem like that big of a deal to me."

I tried to remain calm, making sure I didn't come across hostile. Slowly and through gritted teeth, I explained that the employee would know, and if the employee filed a complaint, then that would cause us a great deal of trouble, legal, monetary, and otherwise. Besides, classifying the employee correctly is the right thing to do.

Once again, Lauren and Larry were visibly frustrated with me. I held my patience. By the time the meeting had ended, we'd all agreed to classify Sam correctly.

I left feeling exhausted, angry, and upset. Every day is a constant battle with them to just do the right thing. Almost every request, proposal, or action by both of them is designed to achieve some personal agenda. They're willing to take advantage of employees, cut corners, and manipulate every situation to get what they want and not what is best for the company. It's a miracle we continue to make money.

This could be a healthy and rewarding place to work. I enjoy people – helping them, mentoring them, and showing them ways that they can advance themselves personally and professionally. That's why I got into Human Resources in the first place.

I sat in my office for the next thirty minutes thinking, "How much more of this can I take?"

People who find themselves forced to file complaints will find their issues treated fairly here. Most days I feel as though I have helped someone. I wouldn't still be here if that weren't the case.

Maddie, my 2:00pm meeting, arrives a little early. She's visibly nervous. After a couple of minutes of chit-chat I ask her how I can help. She hesitates.

"I need to report something I think is against our policy," she says.

Uh oh. This could go one of two ways. Either Maddie is the "someone took my last Diet Coke from the fridge" type (you wouldn't believe how often this happens), or, and that is a big "or," there is a legitimate issue. I tell her that it's my job to listen and encouraged her to share. She says she was scared to mention it because of the people involved.

Immediately I felt the exhaustion return – I've turned into the de facto ethics police around here. I brace myself.

"I was in the office late last week and was walking through the executive suite. When I passed by the president's office I looked in to see that inside was the president's chief of staff, Jason," she says, and then she pauses.

"Maddie, it's okay," I say. "This is a safe place."

She slowly starts to begin again.

"Well, behind him was Lauren, rubbing his shoulders. Lauren was bending over and talking to him like she was whispering in his ear."

"What happened next?" I asked.

"Oh, nothing!" Maddie exclaimed. "I was mortified. I looked away quickly, went back to my office. I don't think I was seen."

"That's quite a story," I say.

I thought she had finished, but Maddie had more to tell. The next day, she asked a colleague in her department if Lauren and her husband were still together.

"Yes," the colleague replied. "But I hear she's sleeping with Jason."

"Thank you, Maddie, for your candor."

I took down the notes and assured her that her name would not be used anywhere, and an investigation would be undertaken to make sure that the company's policies were being followed. I believe she left more or less confident.

My mind reeled. According to our policy, I had to meet with Lauren, Jason, and Larry about this issue. Part of me really wanted to ignore this and pretend I hadn't heard any of it "officially." I had heard some of it through the grapevine, but no one had come in to see me about it. Now, it was no longer a rumor.

Lauren always has Larry's ear. In the past he has defended her bad behavior, made excuses for her, and shown obvious favoritism. Was it because of her alleged relationship with Jason? Or could it be she had a relationship with Larry as well?

Case in point: Lauren had used a company car to go skiing with her sister in Vermont. When it came up, Larry covered for her by saying she met with a client. We don't have any clients in Vermont.

Then at one point last spring, I noticed that every time Jason was out of town on business, Lauren was too. At the time, I didn't think much of it. It seemed much more relevant now. I knew I shouldn't be thinking like this, but they were impossible to avoid. Still, I have to be impartial. I have to do an investigation by the book. I felt scared and hesitant. I hated feeling that way. No one should be fearful at work.

Pursuing the matter wasn't going to be comfortable. It could be dangerous for me and my family. If I was perceived by Larry to be attacking Lauren or Jason with an anonymous report, I might be fired.

Larry understands my value, though. I am hard-working, and I get things done. But I am far from someone he likes or favors. It is unlikely that he would fire me but he could make life very difficult, either directly or indirectly.

A call from my assistant brought a little good news: my last meeting of the day was cancelled. I could leave the office shortly before 5:00 and go home to try and relax.

Miranda and my son Bryan arrived home around 6:30pm after soccer practice bearing take-out from his favorite place. Bryan ran to shower and Miranda asked me what had been going on today.

"There had been a legal issue discussed this morning with a few of the 'usual suspects,'" I said. (I didn't mention Lauren and Larry by name at home.) "They'd even discussed breaking the law if the consequences were tolerable."

She laughed and rolled her eyes.

"Isn't that typical? Did they finally come around and do the right thing?" she asked.

"After some prodding, yes they did," I said.

"Good job, sweetheart," she said.

"There was more," I said. "It's personnel-related and I can't really talk about it. It could cause problems for us both if I push it. Jobs are on the line."

"Can I guess?" she asked.

"Nope, 'fraid not," I said.

She shrugged.

"All we can do is pray about it and do our jobs. We can't control other people," she said.

"By the way, I heard that Lauren is cheating on her husband."

She winked and walked into the kitchen. Bryan came back downstairs all cleaned up and we sat down for a family dinner over pad thai.

I tried to be present at dinner. I tried to show I was listening, and that I cared. But I kept thinking that rumors of the affair were now widespread. This had to be addressed – and quickly. It doesn't take long for employee morale to tank in this kinds of situations. Sometimes

I feel like I am the only one in leadership who actually cares about our employees and this company.

After dinner, my patience gone, I scheduled individual appointments with Lauren and Jason for the following day. If it needed additional reporting to Larry, I would address that at the time. Both Jason and Lauren accepted immediately. I felt relieved that I would not have to fight to get face time.

From the moment I opened my eyes the next morning, I was thinking about the meetings. I had also woken up twice in the middle of the night.

Showering, it occurred to me just how much fear was associated with my job. I was scared of what Larry might do. He was quite capable of being unethical and unfair. As much as I love the work, the people at the top are not people I want to be around. A saddening thought. I was caught between my colleagues and my own need to do the right thing.

A quiet breakfast followed with the family. Miranda is a rock for me, if not for her I think I might lose it sometimes. She really keeps my stress and perspective in check.

I intentionally picked afternoon times for the meetings so that I could use the morning to prepare. Arriving at work, I got a cup of tea and shut myself in.

First, I carefully outlined what I would share with Lauren and Jason, then developed the questions I would ask and thought about what their responses might be. I expected the worst from her and probably something more reasonable from him.

My expectations proved correct. At the meeting with Lauren, I explained carefully what was reported, what the company policy required in response to such a report, and asked for her response.

Naturally, she said nothing of the accusations.

"I can't believe you'd say such a thing. How could you even dignify this ridiculous report with an investigation?" she asked.

"I have to file a report on any complaint that comes from another employee, Lauren. I have to remain entirely impartial," I said.

"Well, you can bet Larry will hear about this immediately," she said.

Before leaving she had some final words.

"You wouldn't pursue this kind of complaint about anyone else, and you know it!" She thought I was waging some kind of personal attack.

"This is my job," I said. "I'm supposed to find the truth. I'll ask again, would you like to respond to the allegations?"

She ignored me and continued ranting.

"I'm being persecuted!" she said. When she finished talking I acknowledged her concerns.

"I assure you, I will conduct this investigation by the book no matter who is involved. I'm meeting with Jason next," I said.

It was clear she was going straight to Larry's office.

Jason and I met in the conference room. He listened intently as I explained what had been reported, what the policy required, and why I was there.

"Jason, there's been reports of some indecent interactions between you and Lauren," I said. "This wouldn't necessarily carry a penalty, but we do need to have this cleared up and ensure the office is a safe place and inoffensive to everyone."

Once I was finished, he sat quietly for a few minutes.

"It happened. The report is true," he said.

I can't say I was shocked it happened, but I never thought he would be this forthcoming.

"So, tell me what happened, Jason," I said.

"I swear, it's completely platonic," he said. "I guess I could see how someone might take it out of context, though. We're just very close."

"Would you like to add anything else?" I asked, as I continued taking notes.

"I've heard the rumors going around about us. They aren't true, though. I think Lauren may be spreading them herself to cover up her affair with Larry."

I had entered a daytime soap opera.

"Thank you for being so honest, Jason," I said. "It makes my job a hell of a lot easier."

"You're welcome," he said.

"I just ask that you exercise better judgement when it comes to physical contact with any employee."

He nodded.

Returning to my office, I documented my meetings and waited for the inevitable call from Larry. About an hour later my phone rang. It was Larry's assistant asking if I could come over.

I had no idea what to expect. But I also knew it would invariably be my fault.

Larry was behind his desk and I took a seat facing him.

"I got an upsetting phone call from Lauren about a meeting you had with her this morning," he said.

I said I was sorry she was upset and explained what the meeting was about. I offered him a copy of my notes. He glanced at them and set them aside.

"I've talked to Jason," he continued. "He assures me that this was not what it looked like and that it won't happen again."

I told him that Jason had told me the same and I agreed. He made no further comment about his talk with Lauren, her side of the story, or any of the threats and accusations she had leveled at me.

He sat back in his chair and said, "Is there anything else?"

"No," I said.

"Thanks. Have a good weekend," he said, without emotion.

That was it. Larry had restructured the entire incident to become a matter about Jason and me. By all accounts, Lauren had almost nothing to do with it. *Teflon.*

Two things were clear: First, I would face no retribution from Larry. Second, it was implicit that I leave it alone. Oh, a third thing, I am sure I can expect even more cold shoulder and resistance from Lauren from here on out.

Once again I left the office fearful of what things would be like in the next leadership team meeting. As I said, I love the work, but the constant tension from attempting to manage these personalities feels near impossible.

I arrived home to find Miranda cooking away and Bryan playing on my iPad. Miranda asked me how it went. I described it to her in the most negative terms possible.

"Hey! You did your best. You can't control them, and it isn't your job to save the world. Would you like some tea?" she asked.

Reflection

1. Are you aware when you get very frustrated?

2. Have you ever been in a similar situation? How did you handle it?

3. Are you focused on being ethical in your work?

4. Are you happy in your job? If not, what is preventing your happiness?

5. Would you leave your job is you weren't happy and weren't respected?

Chapter 17

Chris: Marked By a Difference

I'm comfortable with myself.

I'm going to be late," I think, grabbing my orientation folder. "I've got to stop hitting Snooze." In my rush to get ready I nick myself while shaving in the shower.

"Ugh. Looks like it's pants today after all."

When I was counting sheep last night I was trying to decide what I should wear – pants or a skirt, maybe even a dress. What sends the best message? Well, with a Band-Aid on one leg, I have no choice – it's going to be the black pantsuit. That should send the "I'm a woman to be taken seriously" message. I look in the mirror and tussle my hair. Okay, not the look I was going for, but it'll have to do.

When I decided to go back to school to get my master's degree I never thought that I'd be questioning my career path, or my life in general for that matter. I've always been pretty straight-laced. No drugs, very little drinking, certainly no smoking. This has led me to lead a fairly boring life. I rarely go out, choosing instead to stay in and watch Netflix or read.

Because of all these mitigating circumstances, I've never even had a real, long-term relationship. I always wonder if I'll even get married. But now I have a new lease on life. I look at myself differently. I am happy and starting fresh.

10 minutes into my commute and I'm naturally stuck in gridlock. Traffic. I'm already nervous about meeting everyone, especially my boss. Will she hover over me, making sure that all "my people" are doing their work? Does she have an ear for gossip? All I want is for her to just let me do my job. I really don't want to be micromanaged. Moving from a middle school to a non-profit is going to be a real culture shock. But like I said, I'm ready.

The principal at my former school was the one who suggested I look into a non-profit management degree.

"It could be something useful for the school, not to mention your career," he said. "Writing grants for various initiatives, organizing fundraisers for class field trips, and managing all the new technology that schools constantly recycle. You'll be perfect," he said.

It would certainly be different. As it turned out, it was actually quite refreshing. My courses included people from different non-profit agencies with a wide range of experience. I learned a lot from them, and, in turn, I believe they learned a lot from me.

Who knew I could be a resource? But with my years in education and childhood development, my insight seemed to be invaluable for non-profits geared for children.

I finally pulled into the office complex, finding a spot under the trees outside the office. I closed my eyes and assured myself that this was a new beginning.

"Everything will be okay. You finally have energy to devote to your career again," I said aloud.

That quiet moment ended with a rapping on my window and a kind voice chirping, "Good morning!"

Michelle, the executive director was standing outside my car, with a coffee in hand and a smile on her face, looking in. I had parked right next to my boss without realizing it.

I must've looked so weird sitting there talking to myself," I thought.

"Hi, Chris! You ready for your first day?" She greeted me with a hug as soon as I stepped out of the car.

She was quite cheerful and the hug was, well, oddly reassuring. We chatted as we walked in about how first weeks can be so overwhelming – meeting new people, filling out all of that lovely paperwork. But she was glad to have me "on board," as she put it.

It was going to be different having an eight to five. Being a teacher, we only worked 40 hours a week, but I was usually there by six in the morning and typically did not leave until after five. This was usually followed by either evening classes to complete my degree or grading at home. Maybe this is why I haven't had a decent relationship (any relationships for that matter) in the last few years. A career with a less strenuous schedule, one centered on adults, not the – how do I put this nicely –"delightful" activities and schedules of children will be a welcome change of pace. Now I would have the freedom to be me.

Our office is way down in one of those old, downtown buildings with the cool architectural details and an art deco feel. Everyone was located on the fourth floor of the building, but the hiring of new employees (myself included) had required some of the top layer (e.g. my boss) to move to a space on the first floor.

We have just over 50 employees – not huge, but big enough for me. As we approached the main desk, Michelle told the woman sitting there to ring for Benjamin. She then gave me a quick hug before disappearing into a large conference room on the first floor. Without a word, the woman at the desk was on her phone and before I knew it Benjamin was behind me with a friendly "Hello."

Benjamin was the Human Resources Coordinator in charge of new-hire training. We went to a small room on the fourth floor where I glanced at a glossy folder full of paperwork. He said we were waiting on a few others and excused himself. Looking around I saw a security camera and as nonchalantly as possible, I opened the folder and began pretending to flip through it.

I put the folder down, and spent the next five minutes drumming my nails on the conference table in the increasingly claustrophobic room. As three other new employees walked in, Benjamin formally welcomed us to the organization. He said he had a lot of information to share, and welcomed questions at any point during orientation.

"Don't hesitate to ask me anything," he said.

He was quite enthusiastic, which is probably why he was doing employee training and in HR in general. We all introduced ourselves and said a few words about our new positions and our backgrounds. One of the men had just gotten married, another had just had a baby, and the woman beside me had just gotten engaged to her high school sweetheart.

I thought for a second, and blurted out: "I'm single." I received a few blank stares, and then there was a burst of laughter. (Phew. I took a sigh of relief.) It helped ease any nervous tension, but I still felt out of place.

I drifted in and out as Benjamin explained all the paperwork. "Why is he Benjamin instead of Ben?" I thought. I knew a guy in college who always went by Christopher instead of Chris. That always annoyed me.

As the informational training was wrapping up, we talked about benefits for spouses and children and then about the organization's pet insurance. The latter was a bit more interesting for me.

Later that week we would have an opportunity to meet with Benjamin to craft our package.

I looked at my watch and to my surprise it was lunch time. I was drained already. I got up to stretch my legs and find my office, even though no one had told me where to go. The only things on the desk were a nice desktop computer and a laptop. A blank canvas.

"Hi. I'm Andy," came a welcoming voice from behind.

"Hi, Andy. Nice to meet you," I said. I extended my hand.

"I'll be working for you. I'm in charge of all new client partnerships."

He was a tall, young man with a burst of friendly energy. Although he came in and sat down (somewhat uninvited), he made up for it with his helpful and interesting style. He had just been promoted into the position, he said. After Andy left, I decided I better get lunch.

That's when Abby appeared in my doorway. Beautiful, with red hair, and fresh out of college.

"Hi, I'm Abby."

"Hi, Abby. Nice to meet you!" I said.

"I'll be your right-hand woman and office assistant," she said.

"Thanks. That sounds great!" I said.

She had a real go-getter attitude – I could tell just by looking at her. Her remarks were brief and ended with a promise to update me on all the upcoming meetings when I had a few minutes.

As I was walking to the elevator, a man yelled down the hall, "Hey, you! Lady! Are you the new manager?"

"John the tech guy," as I would later know him as, told me my computer login and password would be ready to go by the time I got back from lunch. As the doors shut on the elevator, I took a deep breath. This really was starting to get overwhelming.

When I returned after having Cobb salad and ice cream, I stepped out of the elevator as Andy was stepping in. He smiled, looked me up and down, and said, "We need to get some color in those clothes!"

I must have had a puzzled look, but there was no time to talk because someone behind me was tapping me on my shoulder, saying: "Excuse me. Miss? Excuse me." I turned to find a short blonde woman telling me Michelle was in her office and hoping I had a few minutes to talk with her about how my day was going. Claire told me I shouldn't take offense at any of Andy's comments. "He's gay, and you know how gay men are." I laughed, but then I felt guilty that I had.

Michelle and I had a good conversation, or at least I think so. I think she understood that I was quite overwhelmed by all of the "new girl" activities of the day.

"Claire and I have worked together for 10 years. She knows the place top to bottom," she said. "You two will be working together."

***

Back home, I put on an old t-shirt and some soft sweatpants, popped a bag of popcorn, and poured a glass of wine. I really needed to look over all of the benefits information so I could get it taken care of the next day. There must have been at least 50 pages in that folder. Flipping through them, I remembered he said the employee handbook is online. Now if I could only remember my username and password – all typical information and nothing out of the ordinary. Medical plan, dental, vision, retirement plans (flip, flip, flip). I knew what I had in the past, so I just circled the plan closest to that.

Then I saw it: "Domestic Partnership Eligibility," – definitely not something I would have come across in the conservative school district I worked for. I instantly thought of Andy, and I wondered if he was dating or living with anyone. It was surprising all the forms you needed to "prove" your relationship. Isn't that counterproductive to being an inclusive workplace?

***

"Beep! Beep! Beep! Beep!"

I can't believe it's already morning. With first day jitters out of the way, I was again excited to be going to work. I got to the office a little early to prepare for my meeting with Benjamin. I signed in to my computer (John the tech guy put my username on a sticky in one of my office drawers), pulled up the company handbook, and began to scan, looking for something to ask Ben.

It appears that we're an inclusive workplace environment. We even have a diversity committee, which was a pleasant surprise. Then I looked at the sexual harassment and discrimination section, an area I've unfortunately had to report on the past. Sometimes people just don't know when to stop or when they've gone too far.

The policies here look good, but surprise! Sexual orientation discrimination is not addressed. According to the handbook, discrimination was only based on sex, gender, race, age, religion, disability, and veteran status. So I could be protected from discrimination as a woman, but not as a lesbian? What if the wrong person found out that I wasn't sure about my sexuality? I don't think I'm totally straight, but I'm not sure I'm lesbian either. Maybe bi? In any case, it looks like there are limits to the organization's nondiscrimination policy.

Both Andy and the comment Claire made yesterday about him were on my mind. It made me uneasy even though I know it was made in joking fashion. I don't know why I'm so concerned about this. It's not like I'm out. In fact, I still don't even know what I am.

Abby came in with a cup of coffee in hand and said Benjamin was ready for me. He was on the phone but waved me in. He must have been talking with a family member because when he said, "Bye," he said, "I love you, too." His office had a few photos, one with him and another woman, one with a dog. I asked him about the domestic partner benefits and why it was so difficult to ensure "proof." He explained that it was a legal matter and could be something the company could bypass.

"Then they might think everyone would be claiming to be in a domestic partnership, though," he said, laughing.

He pointed at the photo of him and another man and said, "My partner and I have been together seven years, and we're legally married in New York. In order for it to be recognized here, and in this workplace, we have to be married in this state, too. And even when that happens – and there will be a day, I know there will be a day – it will take time. I mean, I'm a gay human resources associate, and I still hear the wisecracks and gay slurs. There isn't a lot we can do when the leadership says they won't include sexual orientation and gender identity as protected classes until the federal government declares them to be protected."

Wow, I never knew that these weren't federally protected classes! I guess I came to the right person. We talked for a long time about all of this; I had never needed to think about this in relation to the workplace before. I then asked about inclusiveness in the mission statement.

"We are inclusive all right. I mean, we have pet insurance, right? You just have to wait and pick your battles."

Later that evening I finished all of my benefit information online. At every step of the paperwork I thought about Andy and Benjamin and how their sexual orientation had to be hidden. For example, when I selected medical insurance I was prompted to select for a spouse or children. If I selected spouse, it would have asked for your date of marriage.

When enrolling in my 401(k), I had to enter beneficiaries and the only options were parents, children, spouse, siblings, or other. I could not imagine having to mark my significant other as "other." Even in an organization that proclaims its inclusive mission, their LGBTQ employees are held back in so many ways. Little did I know that I was working for an organization that was hiding discrimination behind buzzwords like "equality" and "inclusion."

***

Things have been going well in the first month on the job. I've been surprised by how much I've enjoyed getting to know my co-workers. But I've also been surprised by how reluctant I've been to share much about myself. This new phase in my life is exciting and full of possibilities, but it's also scary. Now there are questions in my mind about a lot of things that I always took for granted before. Like how I always told myself that I wasn't into relationships because my work was supposedly more important. Now I'm not so sure.

Maybe I've been hiding behind my work as a way of avoiding some really tough questions that come with relationships – like the fact that I can't even remember the last time I was interested in a guy. Shouldn't someone my age have figured all that out by now?

Well, no time to think about that this morning. We've got our first fundraising campaign up and running and I'm knee-deep in correspondence with potential donors. I'm drafting a letter to one of our biggest contributors, Mary Adams Klein. She's made a name for herself across the state for her philanthropy in the arts and in health care. She has been asking us some fairly pointed questions about our organization's commitment to inclusion and social justice. I've been grappling with myself.

Despite the fact that I have these same questions for my employer, I'm trying to explain to her how much work we do to even the playing field and eliminate inequalities in the community. The truth is, however, we don't even have our act completely together when it comes to treating our own people equally. The extra paperwork to get domestic partner benefits, the bias toward heterosexual couples in our medical coverage and retirement accounts – these are just two things that have really started to eat at me the last few weeks.

To top it off, I still hear little comments from various co-workers almost every week that just get under my skin. Just last week there was an LGBTQ Pride Festival at the state capital. Even though we are about an hour away, it was impossible to avoid seeing event posters at bus stations or ads in the paper. On the way to lunch last week, John made a comment about gay pride.

"I've never understood why they need to have 'Gay Pride.' I mean, really, we don't have 'Straight Pride,' do we? And if we did, we'd catch hell for it. Why can't we be proud about being straight?" he asked as his rant came to an end.

I wasn't sure how to respond, but I felt my face flush.

"They just like to flaunt their stuff. It may be overly sexualized or flaming or whatever, but what are you going to do? That's how they are," Claire responded.

I completely lost the ability to form coherent thoughts.

"My God, what if they knew? What would they think of me? Would they still invite me to lunch?" My mind was racing.

The following Monday, Benjamin popped in my office to ask me to serve on the Diversity Committee. Diversity Committee? Well, OK. I do think it's important that we are as inclusive as possible, and I've definitely seen some things that concern me – places where I'm sure we could do better. But I've also seen a lot of things that are great – like the racial diversity here and the fact that we have so many women in respected leadership positions.

Benjamin is still standing in front of me waiting for my answer "Yeah, sure. That would be great," I hear myself saying.

"Wonderful!" he says with a big smile. "They meet every other Wednesday from 2:00 to 3:30 in the main conference room."

Benjamin gives me a brief rundown on the other committee members. Amanda is head of accounting and a close, long-time friend of Michelle's, David works in marketing, and Sunil is the director of community outreach.

"The primary objective is to recruit more minority employees and to ensure we're complying with equal opportunity laws," he says.

***

Wednesday afternoon rolls around and I find myself sitting at a conference table facing Claire, whom I now know fairly well. I can't say the same about David and Amanda, though. David is preoccupied with his iPhone – he must be putting out fires somewhere. Whatever it is, he looks harried.

Amanda, on the other hand, seems totally present and put together. I introduce myself.

"I'm Amanda," she says. "I'm sorry we haven't met earlier."

"Oh, well thank you! I am too. I've been really busy getting adjusted," I say frantically.

The first meeting goes smoothly. Benjamin reports that some new artwork from a local African-American artist has been hung in the main entry. Other than that, the committee spends a decent amount of time filling me in on their recent activities and decisions. It seems as though they all work fairly well together. Our discussion seems more or less open and spontaneous, although David still doesn't seem fully engaged.

The meeting ends with me still worried if or how to bring up my concerns about sexual orientation, especially knowing Claire's habit of saying some questionable things. Amanda seems remarkably sharp. She has a way of communicating with the group that makes us feel good about the work we're doing, and she's clear about why we're doing it.

"I'm glad you're on this committee now," Amanda says, approaching me at the end of the meeting. "Would you like to get coffee later this week? To chat more?"

I'm struck by how she looks at me – it's as if she's looking deep inside of me, seeing things no one else does. It's comforting, but also a little unnerving at the same time.

***

The next day starts with a phone call from Mary Adams Klein. She is intrigued by our latest project.

"To help school systems find innovative ways to root out bullying and build positive social environments is an absolute must," she says. "May we ask a few questions about it?"

"Please do," I say.

"I didn't see anything specific about protecting homosexual teens in your preliminary plans," she says. "What will your project do to address homophobia in schools?"

I'm horrified that gay youth – or teens perceived to be gay – are one of the primary targets for harassment and bullying in schools.

"And not only that," she adds. "But these children, in response to this bullying and harassment, are three to four times more likely than straight children to attempt suicide."

She really knows her stuff.

"Our project will serve the well-being of all students by creating programs and instilling conflict resolution skills among faculty and students," I tell her. "The needs of LGBTQ kids will be included."

She seems unconvinced as we conclude but she agrees to more conversations. I must admit – I wasn't ready for this line of questioning. I make a promise to myself to seek out a comprehensive plan.

When my coffee date/meeting rolls around, I'm ready to get out of the office. I head down to the foyer, and a minute later she comes strolling around the corner with a big smile. She greets me with a hug – which reminds me a little of Michelle – and we decide to walk down the street to a funky little coffee shop. As we walk, she asks about my day, and I start telling her about Mary Adam Klein's concerns about the anti-bullying initiative.

"I wish someone would have thought about how these kids were treated when I was in school," Amanda says. "I took a lot of crap from other students for being a little dyke."

I'm stunned. She's a lesbian? Not only that, but she calls herself a "dyke?"

We place our orders – a latte for me and an Americano for her – and find a table near the window. She seems so comfortable in her own skin. How does she do that? Is it OK for me to ask her about being gay? Damn it, why does this keep coming up? Am I putting out a vibe or something? It's really starting to become a distraction. But I find the words coming automatically out of my mouth: "You were a gay kid?" Amanda laughs in a friendly way. "Yes, and I'm a gay adult, too."

She proceeds to share story after story of her own coming out and lesbian relationships she's had. "I first knew I was gay in high school," Amanda says. "I've been single for over a year now after a nine-year relationship."

I find myself pushing back the urge to tell her about my own self-questioning. She is obviously a safe person as far as being accepting of LGBTQ people, but should I talk about this with someone so high up in the organization? Or with anyone in the organization, for that matter? Wait, she's talking to me about her own journey of self-discovery. So it's okay to reciprocate, right? But what if she thinks that's ridiculous? I realize I'm starting to care about what she thinks of me.

"Oh my God, it's five o'clock already," Amanda says suddenly, glancing at her phone. "I'm so sorry, I think I've monopolized the entire conversation. Please, let's have dinner soon so I can get to know you better."

"Sure! I'd love that!" I say.

The following Monday, Benjamin popped in my office to ask me to serve on the Diversity Committee. Diversity Committee? Well, OK. I do think it's important that we are as inclusive as possible, and I've definitely seen some things that concern me – places where I'm sure we could do better. But I've also seen a lot of things that are great – like the racial diversity here and the fact that we have so many women in respected leadership positions.

Benjamin is still standing in front of me waiting for my answer "Yeah, sure. That would be great," I hear myself saying.

"Wonderful!" he says with a big smile. "They meet every other Wednesday from 2:00 to 3:30 in the main conference room."

Benjamin gives me a brief rundown on the other committee members. Amanda is head of accounting and a close, long-time friend of Michelle's, David works in marketing, and Sunil is the director of community outreach.

"The primary objective is to recruit more minority employees and to ensure we're complying with equal opportunity laws," he says.

***

Wednesday afternoon rolls around and I find myself sitting at a conference table facing Claire, whom I now know fairly well. I can't say the same about David and Amanda, though. David is preoccupied with his iPhone – he must be putting out fires somewhere. Whatever it is, he looks harried.

Amanda, on the other hand, seems totally present and put together. I introduce myself.

"I'm Amanda," she says. "I'm sorry we haven't met earlier."

"Oh, well thank you! I am too. I've been really busy getting adjusted," I say frantically.

The first meeting goes smoothly. Benjamin reports that some new artwork from a local African-American artist has been hung in the main entry. Other than that, the committee spends a decent amount of time filling me in on their recent activities and decisions. It seems as though they all work fairly well together. Our discussion seems more or less open and spontaneous, although David still doesn't seem fully engaged.

The meeting ends with me still worried if or how to bring up my concerns about sexual orientation, especially knowing Claire's habit of saying some questionable things. Amanda seems remarkably sharp. She has a way of communicating with the group that makes us feel good about the work we're doing, and she's clear about why we're doing it.

"I'm glad you're on this committee now," Amanda says, approaching me at the end of the meeting. "Would you like to get coffee later this week? To chat more?"

I'm struck by how she looks at me – it's as if she's looking deep inside of me, seeing things no one else does. It's comforting, but also a little unnerving at the same time.

***

The next day starts with a phone call from Mary Adams Klein. She is intrigued by our latest project.

"To help school systems find innovative ways to root out bullying and build positive social environments is an absolute must," she says. "May we ask a few questions about it?"

"Please do," I say.

"Wonderful!" says Amanda. "How about this Friday, 8:00, at the Reingold?"

"Yeah, let's do it!" I respond. She gives me a big hug before hurrying off in the opposite direction of the office. She must have other things to do tonight, I think. I wander back to my car.

As I settle onto my couch that night, I can't help but think about Amanda, and the fact that I may just have scheduled a date with her.

***

Amanda is the first person I run into the next day. She gives me another big hug and thanks me for spending time with her.

"I hope you don't mind that we never got around to talking business," she says.

"Of course not! I really enjoyed getting to know more about you, and it was good to have a little break from work," I say.

"I don't meet women like you very often, so I thought we should get to know each other," she says.

I smile at the compliment and realize that I'm enjoying this attention. She heads off to her office, and I start walking to mine, thinking about the "women like me" comment.

When I arrive at our 2:00pm, Amanda isn't there yet. Sunil and I talk about unimportant things until Amanda walks in. She says hi to everyone around the table looking at me a little longer. I feel my face go red.

"We need to do something about how gay employees are treated around here," Amanda says.

I can hardly contain my shock. I stare at her for a second, then fumble with my pen.

She looks around the room methodically. Each of us gets a glance from her in turn. Then her eyes land on me and linger.

Is this a test? If I answer "yes," will she and everyone else think I'm gay? If I answer anything but "yes," will Amanda still want to have dinner Friday night? It dawns on me that no one is saying anything, and the silence has become incredibly awkward. As much to end the tension as anything.

"I agree," I say.

Amanda's face brightens and she looks genuinely pleased.

"What do you mean? They're treated just like everyone else," Claire says.

David nods in agreement and looks expectantly at Amanda – and then at me. I'm not sure what to say. I'm just hoping Amanda says something fast. My face is as red as a solo cup by now.

"What I mean is, I've heard a lot of homophobic comments from people in this organization," Amanda explains. "And I think we can do a better job by not being so heterosexist."

"I'm uncomfortable with the fact that sexual orientation isn't included in the company's nondiscrimination policy." (Holy cats, that's me talking – and fast, too.) My anxiety is pretty high by now. Amanda nods in agreement. So does Sunil, to my surprise.

Claire and David still look confused. Have they really been living under a rock? Don't they have any gay friends or relatives? I have forgotten completely about Amanda and what she may or may not think of me.

I'm too pre-occupied by how ignorant David and Claire seem to be. How can I work with people who just don't get it?

Amanda seems much calmer than I am. She enters into a relatively gentle explanation of the differences in civil rights protections between straight people and gay people. She describes how employees in same-sex marriages or partnerships receive different levels of benefits under the organization's current HR policies. David and Claire seem to be listening closely, but they still have confused looks on their faces. Oh my God, people! Why is this so hard to understand? I am so glad Amanda can handle this level of ignorance so well. I am flipping out inside. I want to scream, but I hold it in. I take a deep breath and just listen.

***

Well, Friday has finally arrived. It was a long week, but I made it through. I've done a lot of research into LGBTQ bullying in schools this week, in an attempt to satisfy Mary Adam Klein's requests. I had no idea how bad it is for these kids. Guess I never really thought about it before, since I never thought of myself as gay growing up. True, I wasn't all that into guys, but it didn't seem like any big deal. I was just more into my sports and studies. I dated boys, but nothing too serious. I just didn't realize so many kids were coming out while they were in middle school and high school.

How can they know their sexuality at that young an age when I'm not entirely sure of my own? Lucky kids. But are they? The statistics I read on the bullying and harassment are disturbing – not to mention the elevated suicide rates. Mary is right – we absolutely have to include programming specific to LGBTQ kids in our anti-bullying initiative.

I get home around 6:30pm that night, and realize I only have an hour to get ready. I am genuinely nervous. But also excited. I can't wait to talk to Amanda about how she handled David and Claire. She was so calm. So smooth. And so convincing. How did she do that? Wasn't she fuming underneath it all?

But what I'm really looking forward to is simply seeing her and telling her more about myself. She's safe, understanding, and she seems like someone who won't break confidence.

Amanda is already waiting at a table when I arrive at the Reingold. She fits right in, but I have so rarely eaten at places as fancy as this. As I approach the table, for the first time I appreciate her outer beauty and not just how intriguing she is as a person.

"You handled that meeting so well," I say. "Weren't you furious at David and Claire for being so clueless?"

"Yes, and no," she replies. "I've learned not to take people's beliefs or perspectives personally. They've inherited some limited thinking and haven't yet had those beliefs challenged. I wouldn't be doing myself any favor if I just went off on them. I have to be willing to meet them where they're at if I'm going to have any positive effect on them at all."

"But attitudes like theirs are why the world is so homophobic," I suggest. "I could have just shaken them in that meeting!"

Amanda laughs. "I'm glad you didn't, but I can understand the feeling. It does get old – being the token lesbian, being the only one to speak up on issues like this. At least you said you were with me on trying to change things."

"Yes, I am," I say. "And I may be with you in other ways, too."

"What do you mean?" Amanda asks.

"I've been doing a lot of soul-searching lately," I say after a deep breath. "And I've come to be pretty sure that I'm either lesbian or bisexual."

"You mean you haven't identified as lesbian all along?" Amanda laughs. But it's a friendly laugh, not the mocking one that I was afraid of. "I'm sorry I assumed, but it seems to me that you are clearly not straight."

"Yeah, I'm not straight. That is the one thing I know." I laugh a little and stop to gather my thoughts. "You're the first person I've told that I've been questioning myself. Everyone else in my life knows me as straight."

"You're kidding!" Amanda exclaims. "Wow, this must be a really exciting time for you. Congratulations!"

"Thanks!" I say. "It feels weird, but so good to finally tell someone. Thanks for being someone I can talk to."

"No problem!" says Amanda. "I'm flattered that you chose to talk with me about this. It can be scary at first, but totally worth it. Let's order, and then I want to hear more about your journey."

In that case, we better clear the rest of the evening.

Reflection

1. What is diversity to me? And what do I know about diversity in my workplace?

2. What do I know about the LGBTQQ community in my workplace? How can I learn more?

3. In what ways are the policies, politics, and culture in my workplace heteronormative?

4. What aspects of this should I explore and consider further in order to be a better co-worker?

5. Chris navigates her sexual orientation through this chapter. In what ways have my colleagues and I navigated sexuality in the workplace (such as dress codes, sexual harassment, talking about our significant others, displaying photos in the office)?

6. How do I enter conversations to combat hurtful stereotypes in the workplace?

7. Am I someone my colleagues can trust with secrets?

Chapter 18

Steve: Faith, Failure, and Fortune

My self-confidence, courage, and hard work have paid off.

It was about 7:00pm, and my wife Meagan and I were about to sit down and eat dinner. We heard a loud knock at the front door. I peered through the blinds and saw an Alto County Sheriff's car. Apprehensively, I approached the front door.

"Who is it?" I asked.

"Deputy Williams with the Alto County Sheriff's Department."

I opened the door slowly to reveal a stocky officer peering up at me.

"Steve Smith?" the deputy asked.

"Yes?" I answered.

Immediately he thrust a summons into my hand. A bank was suing me for defaulting on a business loan. This was the first summons I had ever received about business. It would not be the last.

A failed restaurant venture had cost me more than $100,000, or basically all my life's savings. So at the ripe old age of 28 I was facing business litigation. By the time I hit 30 I would be involved in more lawsuits, mediations, and consent agreements than most people face in their entire lives.

You might say I had assumed professional status in the art of dispute resolution. Very quickly I learned what attorneys could and could not do in the realm of business law. I knew exactly how long it could take to sue a business owner, get a judgment, and begin collection efforts. The Sheriff knocking on the door was a little unnerving, but it eventually became such a normal occurrence that I would offer the deputy a glass of cold water on particularly hot days.

So here I was, married, with no business, no money, and a young child. The next three years loomed as the darkest times of my life. I was happy to be married and be a father, but the stress of owing so much money from the restaurant failure was tremendous. To make matters worse, I had pledged my home as collateral for the loan I used to start an Italian restaurant. Despite the fact that I never had any restaurant experience, I couldn't cook, and I wasn't Italian. Think Bill Gates, sans computers.

Failing at something or losing a lot of money can make you feel deeply inadequate. After all of the hoopla associated with our grand opening, I was embarrassed. I was ashamed to go out with friends and often went the other way when I saw people I knew. I felt like everyone was looking at me and laughing. I continually wondered what my next step would be, and I walked around with my head down for about a year after the restaurant failed. I did nothing but mope. It took a full three years before I straightened out all of my finances.

Meagan and our two little girls kept me going. Family is the most important thing in life. Yes, absolutely there were times that I wanted to quit. But fortunately, I had someone there to cheer me on and encourage me to keep going.

My faith helped too. Not just in a religious sense, but in an absolute sense. Faith in God, faith in people, faith in systems, faith in employees. I was quickly learning that in order to be an entrepreneur, I had to have absolute faith in all these things. No one can do it alone.

Through this whole ordeal I learned that faith and failure actually work together. Failure is life's way of providing feedback.

Like most people, I was not inclined to hear feedback and criticism. It's odd that something so common in our lives, an event repeated over and over since birth, can still be so loathsome. We all fail at something in our lives, perhaps numerous times. Even our first steps when we were babies comes after dozens of falls. If you haven't taken a fall, must be reading this on the floor.

Society seems to focus sharply on the successful entrepreneur. When I think about entrepreneurship, I think of Steve Jobs, Oprah Winfrey, Robert Johnson, Ted Turner, or John D. Rockefeller. We always seem to associate entrepreneurship with the hugely successful. They made millions, if not billions, of dollars. Today many successful entrepreneurs are very young, thanks to the explosion of the Internet and the many technical applications that it spawned.

These rockstar entrepreneurs are the exception, not the rule. If you had to reach billionaire status to start your own business, I wouldn't have had a chance. Most of the successful entrepreneurs that I've met are people who had a desire to create a better quality of life and a more comfortable lifestyle. Like them, I wanted to be in control of my destiny and chart my own course.

I was not a multi-millionaire by the time I was 18, and I certainly did not start an Internet software company from my college dorm while eating pizza in my pajamas.

In fact, over the last 25 years I have had almost as many different hourly or salaried jobs. These jobs almost always ended one of two ways. I either simply said, "I quit." Or, the boss said, "You're fired." Financial services, insurance, food service, clothing, retail, telemarketing, marketing telephones. You name it, I've done it. One summer I even sold encyclopedias door to door, when that was "a thing." It was easily the worst job I ever had. I went through two pairs of shoes and ended up at most of my appointments drenched in sweat – and that was only to deliver the A-M volume. That is when I realized I didn't want to work for anyone but myself.

One of my earliest exposures to entrepreneurship came from my uncle George, who lived in Chicago and decided to open a haberdashery on the south side of Chicago called Esquire Menswear. *Esquire* was a popular men's magazine, one that is still in circulation today and is actually a TV channel. He gave all his shares of stock in the company to all of his nieces and nephews, me included. When he told me that I owned 10 shares of stock in Esquire Menswear, I was elated. I distinctly remember the pride that I felt in knowing that I owned something. You would've thought that I was Donald Trump when you heard me talking to my seven and eight-year-old buddies. I owned something, and I knew that it was valuable – even if I couldn't touch it or sell it for cash.

That was the beginning of what has become a lifelong commitment to and interest in entrepreneurship. There is nothing – absolutely nothing – that fills your spirit with as much pride as owning and controlling my own business.

One hot summer day, I was eight, and engaged in the third most popular religion in the wetlands of Missouri: crawdad fishing.

I learned how to catch them by baiting a small paper clip with a worm, dropping it in a hole, and slowly pulling them up to catch the crawdad. One day a seasoned 14-year-old friend, Tom Flint, showed me another way.

"You gotta trawl the bottom," Tom said. "That's where they all are anyway."

I had an idea. I would catch as many crawdads as I could can and sell them. So I gathered all of my seven and eight-year-old comrades and created my first business plan on the back of a paper grocery bag. The plan was simple: 1) Use the rake. 2) Collect crawfish. 3) Bring them to my house. 4) Go door to door to take orders and sell them for 10 cents each. 5) Profit!

By my modest calculations we could catch at least 100 a day, which would have netted me (excuse the pun) $10 a day. This was a small fortune in 1978, and more than enough to keep the entire neighborhood happy with candy, potato chips, and soda.

Plenty of kids wanted to work. All they needed was a rake, something that rural communities have an abundance of. I dug a huge hole near the side of my house and filled it with water. If you're nodding your head in agreement with simple genius of this plan, you're right. It was pretty damn good.

In one week's time, everyone was working and I was riding around on my bike ensuring that production was well underway (a managerial prodigy, if I do say so myself). We hauled buckets of crawfish back and forth between the ditches and the storage hole. Things were going great.

By mid-day we had surpassed 100 crawdads, but due to the blistering sun our parents forced us in for a break. Two or three hours later, we reconvened at the CSC, or Crawdad Storage Central. To our amazement our prized crustaceans were nowhere to be found. Had we been robbed? Perhaps we were the victim of a crawfish conspiracy, meant to take down the little guy to ensure the profits of the big-wig crawfish corporation.

A survey of the surrounding area gave us the answer. Our crawfish decided the stagnant water in the storage hole that I dug was too hot for them, so they decided to crawl out and return to the cool flowing ditches. How all of them found their way back there, I have no idea.

It never really occurred to me that I hadn't dug the hole deep enough or the sides steep enough. In two hours time my potential profits vanished back into muddy water, along with the morale of my workforce. Thankfully my parents had an ample supply of popsicles to pacify my comrades.

Given the economic blight and distress in this Missouri town, my parents decided that it was best for us to move to St. Louis in search of better opportunity. My parents had different perspectives on how to do that. My mother thought an advanced education ending in a law degree was the way. My father thought that pursuing entrepreneurship and real estate ownership would lead to success. Unfortunately, when two married people don't agree on the direction that they should take as a couple, the result can be disastrous.

My parents divorced when I was very young. I immediately became a child raised alone by a single mother. My father was still very much in the picture, but the strength and security of our family was gone.

We eventually moved to Kansas City, where I completed high school at Barstow. I did quite well and was admitted to several leading colleges, eventually settling on Morehouse College in Atlanta. While there, I continued my entrepreneurial ventures by selling snacks out of my dorm room and hocking graphic tee shirts. I graduated with a respectable GPA – not quite Magna Cum Laude, but Thank You Laude. That was good enough for me. Rather than go the corporate route like many of my peers did after graduation, I moved to Washington, D.C. to stay with family.

While in D.C., a family friend, my cousin, and I decided that we should take a shot at starting a business. Mike, the family friend, was a barber and had created an idea for a product for hair stylists. I provided the business acumen and administrative expertise, while Mike provided the industry knowledge. So at 23 I started my first legitimate business venture. For me, "legitimate" meant that we filed articles of incorporation, opened bank accounts, and paid taxes. Your definition may differ to such qualities as, oh, I don't know, profitability? We also secured a patent on our product – no easy task. We even went through the exercise of creating molds and having our product manufactured. After about a year we had sold several thousand units. That may sound impressive, but it wasn't enough for us to become the millionaires that we thought we would after the first year.

We soon found that reputable distributors and suppliers were scarce. We didn't have the ability to sell on a receivables basis. What this meant was that our business was forced to shut its doors after only a couple of years. It was a great experience, and one I really learned a lot from about patents, trademarks, manufacturing, sales, and marketing. I used to view difficulty and setbacks with a certain resentment, but as I mature, I have come to see how all experiences like that have shaped me into the entrepreneur, businessman, and leader that I am today.

To date, I have started and closed more businesses than I care to remember – at least six or seven formal business entities and dozens of business ideas that you might call "side hustles." It's hard work.

Today, I own three main businesses, all of which are rooted in things that I am passionate about: concessions, real estate development, and entrepreneurial education.

Given all of my experiences, including working in corporate America, it seems to me that entrepreneurship is the only way for a person to truly be free and independent with regards to their life pursuits. My feeling is that entrepreneurship is more than just starting a business – it's a strategy, a mindset that can help promote a life full of meaning and purpose.

I am happiest when I am in entrepreneur mode and thinking of new businesses and vetting new ideas.

Benjamin E. Mays, the late president of Morehouse College said, "Every woman or man was born into this world to do something unique, something distinctive, and if he or she does not do it, then it will never be done."

That's pretty powerful when you think about it; only you can do something in particular that God wants done.

Failure has gotten a bad rap. Even saying the word without applying it to any particular situation causes most people to respond in a negative way. But there can be no success without failure.

From mud pools in Missouri, to cops banging my door, trust me, I know a thing or two about it. But here I am.

The old saying from Mary Pritchard goes, "Failure is not falling down. Failure is not getting up again."

It's time to get up.

Reflection

1. Are you a risk-taker? Are you comfortable in taking risk to improve your life?

2. Are you consistent in setting and reaching your personal objectives?

3. Does your desire for personal freedom and flexibility outweigh your desire for money?

4. Is your self-confidence high enough to overcome life's adversities?

5. What do you have a passion for?

6. How is your faith and where do you draw your strength and tenacity from?

Personal Development Plan

How Can <u>You</u> Benefit from These Stories

By now, you know that some of our friends in this book are confused. Others are on their way to confusion. Confusion can be the cause of real difficulty in this world.

It's nothing new. People were desperately confused 2,000, 3,000, even 4,000 years ago.

If they were Chinese, they might have gone to see a sage like Confucius about their confusion. He would have taught them self-restraint, compassion, and caring for others.

Confucius said, "Wherever you go, go with all your heart." That's the opposite of confusion.

If they were Greek and living in Athens, they might have brought their confusion to Socrates, a philosopher whose wisdom and good sense shines forth even today.

"Know thyself," he said. Look at yourself. Understand who you are. You have a lot to offer – to yourself, as well as to the world around you. So take up the challenge of Socrates. "Know Thyself."

My own advice is this: You are the writer of your own life. Start writing.

In other words, you are in control of your own thoughts, feelings, and behavior. Your personal development and growth require a plan based on that fact.

Here's the plan:

1. Increase your Self-Awareness. Recognize your thoughts, feelings, emotions, and behaviors.

- **Keep a Daily Log for 14 Days**. Record after just two conversations what you notice about your thoughts and feelings in these conversations. Make sure you write only about yourself.

- **After the 14 days, start recording at least three conversations a week over the next two months**. What do you notice about yourself? Do you frequently interrupt the other person? Do you make eye contact during the conversation? Do you multi-task during the conversation – looking at your phone, for example? Can you change these habits?

- **Keep a personal Journal.** Every day write one or two paragraphs about what you noticed about yourself throughout the day – your thoughts, feelings, and behaviors. Every three or four months take time to review your personal journal and evaluate what you've learned about yourself.

- **Meditation**. Sit or lay quietly for 10-15 minutes each day – start with long, deep inhale and hold it for 10 seconds; now gently, slowly release your breath and notice the movement of your stomach. Focus on your breathing, causing it to slow down. Focus on the natural rise and fall of the breath. As thoughts come into your mind, allow them to pass without focusing on them by returning to your breathing cycle.

2. Increase Your Self-Control. Manage your own emotions.

- **List your most common emotions** – Do you regularly feel angry, sad, anxious, scared, rage, shame, pity, cruelty, pride, envy, hate, love, joy, etc.

- **Keep a Daily Log for 14 Days**. List any strong emotion you experience and the situation in which it occurs. (Some days you may not show any strong emotions.)

- **Is there a certain situation that rouses an emotion in you?** If so, develop a plan to manage it ahead of time, e.g., meeting with a person who "gets under my skin."

3. Increase Your Social Awareness. Track your interaction with others.

- **Keep a daily log for 14 days.** Record after three conversations what you notice about the other person – their feelings, concerns, needs, and the like. Is he/she a good listener? Does he/she show appreciation? Then over a two-month period record at least three conversations a week.

- **Focus on the other person's behavior**. Do they make good eye contact? Did they ask clarifying questions? Did they listen more than they talked at times? Did they ignore external distractions and remain relatively relaxed? Note their tone of voice, facial expressions, and body language.

- **Improve your listening skills**. How well do you listen? Over a 14 day period, reflect on two conversations you had each day and list the following listening behaviors you performed:
    - **Made good eye contact**
    - **Leaned toward the other person**
    - **Asked clarifying questions**

- Used appropriate non-verbal behaviors, e.g. occasionally nodding, facial expressions to reflect emotions back to the person, etc.
- Remained relatively relaxed – tone of voice, facial expressions, body posture, etc.
- Used open-ended questions
- Ignored external distractions
- Used reflective listening – "It sounds like you are concerned about your finances."
- Did not talk over the person when there are talking

4. Use an Emotional Intelligence Checklist.

Take the following checklist as your own. It will help you to sharpen and maintain your overall people skills. Every third day, mark the following as True or False.

- I listen attentively to others.
  T F

- I feel strong emotions and hold them back.
  T F

- I stay composed and positive, even in trying moments.
  T F

- I start the conversation as a listener first, seek clarity, and learn the person's concerns.
  T F

- I understand what I'm feeling and am able to clearly express my feelings to others.
  T F

- I am aware of my strengths and weaknesses.
  T F

- I seek constructive feedback and incorporate it into my understanding of myself.
  T F

- I do what I say I will do.
  T F

- I treat others with respect regardless of their background
  T F

- I hold myself accountable for my thoughts, emotions and behaviors
  T F

- I believe in myself during the good, the bad, and the ugly times
  T F

Remember, this is a True or False test of yourself. Take it every third day for two months.

Acknowledgements

I'll never forget the time I went with my father to the RC Cola plant in Chattanooga one shining Saturday morning. Dad and I were walking among the huge stacks of cola cases. Everywhere, reaching up to the ceiling, stacks and stacks of cases. Thousands of cans of soda. As a kid, I was in awe.

"I wonder if this is a lifetime supply!" I said to my father. "This must be a great place to work."

He turned to me, gripped my arm, and looked directly into my eyes. "You're not going to work here. You're going to college. Do you hear me?"

"Yes, sir," I responded, my voice shaking. "I'll go to college." At the time, I didn't see why the two were mutually exclusive, and maybe I still don't. But it sure did get me to thinking.

By the time I was a sophomore in high school, I began to realize what he had meant. From then on, my heart was set on getting into a good school. I would be the first in my family to go to college. My two brothers, Mack and Butch, followed suit. At times, all three of us were together at the same university. Both Mack and Butch have since gone on to great careers. Our parents sacrificed for us, never indicating how much they were giving up. A lot, I later found out. Thank you, Mom and Dad, (or, as the world has known you, Aline and Ray Hannah).

I've been fortunate to have great teachers and professors throughout my life as well, starting with my first grade teacher, Ms. Peeples, at Fort Oglethorpe Elementary and on to my doctoral advisor, Dr. Todd Risley, at the University of Kansas. My subsequent years at the Hay Group saw my skills and knowledge increase exponentially, under the guidance of Dr. David McClelland of Harvard University.

My profession has required extensive reading and research about human behavior, organizational performance, and leadership. Besides the Holy Bible, I have gained knowledge from the writings of Dr. Daniel Goleman, Jim Collins, Dr. John Kotter, Dr. Stephen Covey, Peter Drucker, James Kouzes, and Dr. Barry Posner. Of course, my knowledge is not complete without the *Harvard Business Review* and *The Wall Street Journal*.

This book was born out of my work with, and observations of, very talented people who were blessed with an abundance of character. Throughout my time with them, I used my insight to help them manage their good, bad, and ugly life experiences. I then set out to write a "how-to book" to help others learn how to be more emotionally intelligent human beings. After months of research and writing, I asked myself: "Why reinvent what is already available from the authors I read?" I dropped the idea.

About a year later, I reviewed some research about the effectiveness of storytelling in therapeutic situations. That afternoon of reflection in my study planted the seed, both in my heart and in my head. With encouragement and support from my wife Kay, I started the interviews, research, and examination of personal experiences. I also began assembling stories about people dealing with difficult situations in their own lives and careers. Thank you, sweetheart, for nudging me in this direction and for reading the first and second drafts of each chapter.

Soon after I began writing, I realized I would need people who had more knowledge and experience regarding certain subjects. This led me to develop a small team to cover the full spectrum of work and personal life.

That team of contributors have included, in no particular order:

- Whitney Caudill, J.D. – Vice President for University Engagement, Manchester University

- Barb Burdge, Ph.D. – Associate Professor of Social Work, Manchester University

- Pattie Hannah, R.N. – Retired Nurse, Dunwoody, Georgia

- Steven Kroeger – Recent Graduate of Western Kentucky University, Brentwood, Tennessee

- Kevin McGee – Founder/CEO of Avid Entrepreneurship, Atlanta, Georgia

- Timothy McKenna-Buchanan, Ph.D. – Assistant Professor of Communication Studies Manchester University.

To each of you, I am grateful.

I have been careful to include facts rather than value statements, especially on anything that smelled of political positions. To accomplish this, I reached out to the people I trust most.

I want to thank and acknowledge Dr. David McFadden, President of Manchester University; Jon Robertson, Chairman/CEO of UMB Colorado; William Short, CEO of AmeriFlex; Bart McCollumn, President/COO of AmeriFlex; Frank Casagrande, CEO of Casagrande Consulting; Dr. Marylouise Fennell, RSM, Hyatt-Fennell Executive Search; Owen Williams, Ph.D., President of Associated Colleges of the South; Gene Kansas, Owner of Commercial Real Estate Firm & Star of Sidewalk Radio Show on WMLB, Atlanta; and Charles (Butch) Hannah, NFL Game Official and youngest brother.

I have been fortunate to have the people of The Ledlie Group of Atlanta, Georgia, as my editors and advisors: Rand Rozier, Philip Hauserman, and Joseph M.A. Ledlie, brought life to the book. Thanks to all of you.

I'd like to end on a personal note to you, the reader. Thank you for taking the time to read these stories about work and life. Hopefully, as a result, you have become more aware of your own thoughts, feelings, emotions, and behaviors.

Now it's your turn. Go and tell your own story!

Contributing Writers

Kevin McGee

For Kevin, entrepreneurship is more than starting a business. It's a strategy and way of life that helps him live with meaning and purpose. His goal is to help entrepreneurs understand the risks and rewards of their trade by enabling them to make wise decisions that lead to successful outcomes. Over the past 20 years Kevin has helped hundreds of entrepreneurs start, grow, and, when necessary, exit their businesses.

Kevin is the founder of Avid Entrepreneurship, a consulting firm dedicated to helping entrepreneurs build better businesses. He is a graduate of Morehouse College, Atlanta, Georgia.

Kevin was responsible for writing Chapter 18.

Barb Burdge, Ph.D.

In 2003, following several years of professional social work in the field of child welfare, Barb Burdge began teaching social work and gender studies at Manchester University. Her current research as an associate professor revolves around the lived experiences of transgender identities and education for social justice. Barb, her partner, their dogs, and horses live on her family's historic farmstead in rural northern Indiana.

Dr Burdge is Associate Professor of Social Work, Social Work Program Director, Manchester University, and received her Ph.D. from Indiana University.

Barb, alongside Tim, was responsible for writing Chapter 17.

Tim McKenna-Buchanan, Ph.D.

Tim McKenna-Buchanan is an Assistant Professor in the Department of Communication Studies at Manchester University. His research focuses on the intersection of difference (or diversity) and organizational life, with an emphasis on the ways narratives empower identity and the stories that create, maintain, and change individuals' lived experience.

Dr. McKenna-Buchannan's research also extends into the college classroom where he, along with colleagues, explore various interpersonal dynamics in the classroom (i.e. disclosure and emotion). He also teaches in the areas of organizational communication, public relations, and communication ethics.

His work has been published in journals such as Communication Education, Communication Teacher, and Health Communication. Dr. McKenna-Buchannan received his Ph.D in Communication Studies from Ohio University.

Tim, alongside Barb, was responsible for writing Chapter 17.

Steven Kroeger

Steven is currently working as a teaching assistant. He received his B.A. in English and minor in Computer Science at Western Kentucky University. He lives in Brentwood, Tennessee, with his family and dogs.

Steven was responsible for writing Chapter 3.

Pattie Hannah, R.N.

Pattie studied at the University of North Carolina, Middle Tennessee University and received her degree in nursing at DeKalb College, Atlanta, Georgia.

Her nursing career went on to span 24 years, during which time she earned Certifications in Critical and Cardiac Care, Dialysis and Hospice.

The last 12 years of her career were spent caring for patients in hospice settings. Pattie currently lives with Mack, her husband of 44 years, in Dunwoody. Together, they have a daughter, Jennifer, and a son, David, and four exquisite granddaughters. They enjoy traveling, teaching their respective Bible studies, and serving as lay leaders at their church.

Pattie was responsible for writing Chapter 9.

Whitney Caudill, J.D.

Whitney Caudill is the vice president for strategic initiatives and external relations at Manchester University. A licensed attorney, she is also an associate professor teaching pharmacy law and related subjects in the College of Pharmacy. Caudill joined the Manchester University's College of Pharmacy as associate dean for administration and finance in 2011.

As the College of Pharmacy's associate dean, she not only managed its non-academic operations, but was also a key player in the design and construction process of the University's Fort Wayne campus.

She earned a Bachelor of Arts degree in government from University of Virginia and her doctor of jurisprudence degree from University of Tennessee College of Law. She is licensed to practice law in Virginia, Tennessee, and the United States District Court for the Western District of Virginia.

Whitney was responsible for writing Chapters 12, 14, and 16.

About the Author

Gerald T. Hannah, Ph.D.
Advisor to executives across the country and overseas, Jerry Hannah holds a doctorate in behavioral psychology and puts it to work on behalf of others.

From his base in Atlanta as head of a global consulting firm, Dr. Hannah provides executive coaching, leadership development, high-performing team guidance, and succession management planning.

A frequent broadcast guest, he is a public speaker, author, and guest lecturer at colleges and universities. In the U.S. and abroad he works with leaders of corporations, non-profits, and counsels presidents and senior officers in higher education.

Besides heading The Gerald Hannah Group, Dr. Hannah also serves as a senior consultant to Casagrande Consulting and The Hay Group. He and his wife, Kay, live in Atlanta, Georgia.